OPEN
BOOK

A LIBRARIAN'S GUIDE TO ACADEMIC PUBLISHING

OPEN
BOOK

JAMES WISER
and
ROLF A. JANKE

Editors

MISSION BELL MEDIA

FIRST EDITION

Library of Congress Preassigned Control Number
2016916760

ISBN 978-0-9971757-1-4

MISSION BELL MEDIA

Rolf A. Janke, CEO
Sara Tauber, Editorial Manager
Mary Jo Scibetta, Director of Publishing and Marketing Services

—— Contents ——

Introduction

Academic libraries are the central hubs of any campus setting. It is where highly organized content in print or digital formats is available for faculty, students, and the campus community. As this content flows out to every corner of a campus and beyond, one should consider the bigger picture: where did that content come from and how did it get there? Of course, libraries purchase the content, but before that step happens, there is a significant ecosystem of content creation and dissemination and we believe many librarians are wondering how it all fits together. Academic publishers and their partners are behind it all, and the library market with its purchasing power is now more than ever a core customer segment to their financial viability and sustainability. A publishing first, *Open Book* represents an authoritative perspective about the elements, the ideas, the processes, and predictions involved in academic publishing as it relates to the library market and its patrons.

In our travels, it has become increasingly apparent that publishers seem to be learning a lot more about the library, yet, lacking the opportunity, librarians know little of what happens behind the doors of academic publishers and the vendors who play a vital role in distributing their content. Gaining knowledge of the publishing business will perhaps empower you to associate, communicate, and negotiate with them, and by design, create a leadership role for yourself among your peers. As the editors of this book—one a librarian, the other an academic publisher, with a combined 52 years in the academic library space—we feel that this book will also enrich you with authoritative perspectives and commentaries on the most important components of the publishing process and provide insight to how complex academic publishing for the library market really is.

Publishers come in all shapes and sizes, for-profit and not-for-profit, and have strong ties with closely related business such as distributors, e-book aggregators, and societies. One book cannot possibly cover all of the components and services that publishers provide, but we feel that we have captured an excellent core of key topics that are not only relevant today but will be in the future as well. More importantly, we are honored to have a stellar list of contributors who have all forged ground, leading their respective companies and services forward to better serve academic libraries.

More specifically, we start out the book with a look at the publishing industry as a whole, beginning with a comprehensive chapter by Michael Levine-Clark, who, as an academic librarian, sets the tone as to the significance behind publishing ecosystems. He examines the point at which librarians and publishers intersect and how to best build this important relationship. Stephen Rhind-Tutt's chapter follows, with an in-depth look at what qualities make for a good publisher, in the details of the day-to-day business as well as the value of being open to ideas. Stephen looks candidly at the changing market and proposes real-life solutions. Building on the theme of challenges in publishing, Alison Mudditt discusses the important role the university press plays in the advancement of scholarship. Producing this valuable content faces challenges in the form of economic and market changes. Alison describes the collaboration needed to continue this advancement in the future. Offering the flip side of the publishing coin, Barbara Walthall gives us the viewpoint of associations and societies. When deciding whether to self-publish or partner with a publisher, Barbara details clear advice on how to navigate the uncertainty. She offers two case studies that examine the pros and cons of each situation. Following this discussion, Robert Boissy examines a topic that has proven controversial: open access. Robert offers not only the general economic perspectives; he also examines the challenges of the publisher, the author, and the reader. Just as Robert discusses intersecting needs, Mark F. Kendall explains the world of the library monographic service provider. He describes how the needs of the library as well as the needs of the publisher meet in the world of the library service provider, and offers advice on how to gain the most value from this important relationship. James Wiser finishes off the first section of the book with a look at how globalization affects libraries and publishers alike. James looks at real-life examples of how world economics have affected library budgets. He also presents the opposite point of view as he examines how publishers have to react to changes in the global climate.

In the second section, our book focuses on publishing on a microlevel, beginning with Elisabeth Leonard's look at market research. Elisabeth explains market research, product development, and the impacts on the publishing industry. She describes how thoughtful and articulate this research must be and how libraries and publishers can work together to find the best value from this process. Jayne Marks continues the theme of collaboration as she explains the complex world of journals. She describes the various players involved in publishing a journal—the authors, the editors, the societies, the publishers, the librarians, and so on. Although the balance is a difficult one and the amount of work is vast, partnership makes it possible. Steven Smith also describes the complexity of the publishing world as he explains the work of an acquisitions editor. Steven describes the combination of vision and strategy needed in conjunction with the attention to business detail demanded in a changing market. The theme of a changing market is also front and center in Rolf Janke's chapter on reference. To illustrate the point, Rolf examines the transition from print to digital reference. The day-to-day decisions associated with this uncertainty are outlined in a case study of how to create a must-have reference work. The changing climate of the publishing world has affected reference significantly just as technology and economics have affected the e-book. Rebecca Seger delves into this complicated topic by describing the challenges in printing monographs as well as the challenges of digitizing this content. Sales and usage statics are examined as Rebecca joins this information with real-life decisions made daily by librarians. Carol Richman carefully examines details of the publishing industry as she describes copyright, licensing, and how these agreements affect libraries and publishers alike. She examines the complex issues that students, authors, librarians, and publishers grapple with daily. Jenni Wilson wraps up the second section of the book with a look at the world of sales. She offers a glimpse into a world that starts when the publisher meets the librarian. From day-to-day interaction to longstanding relationships, she describes how everyone benefits from a balance between knowledge of the library and knowledge of the publishing world.

We hope that you will find value in what this book has to offer and that you will share some of the insights you have gleaned with your colleagues. Finally, it is our goal that this book will make you an informed librarian by directly bringing you fresh insight about this publishing ecosystem. Enjoy, and perhaps the next time you are at a conference where publishers and vendors are present, take the opportunity to learn more . . . this book is only the beginning.

James Wiser, Editor
Rolf A. Janke, Editor

Acknowledgments

I would like to thank the authors included in this work, as each contributor opened up their daily lives to us and let us walk a mile in their steps. In addition to the editorial talents of the staff of Mission Bell Media, I want to thank so many of my friends in this wonderful industry—both librarians and publishers—all of whom work to disseminate scholarship for the greater good of society. Finally, I want to especially thank Rick Burke, my dear friend, colleague, former boss, and mentor. He models to me what appropriately bridging the gap between librarianship and academic publishing can and should look like, and his life and career have in many ways inspired this work.

James Wiser
Editor

I would like to sincerely thank all of the contributors for their time and creative energy. It was an honor to work with them and I actually learned a great deal myself from reading their chapters. This book would not have been possible without the amazing editorial talents of Sara Tauber and Mary Jo Scibetta. Their dedication and commitment to making this happen was a joy to be involved with. A shout out to Danielle Janke, Mission Bell Media's Social Media Marketing Manager, who as you read this is spreading the word on *Open Book*.

Rolf A. Janke
Editor

List of Contributors

Robert Boissy
*Director of Institutional Marketing
& Account Development - Americas
Springer Nature*

Michael Levine-Clark
*Dean and Director
University of Denver Libraries*

Rolf A. Janke
*Chief Executive Officer
Mission Bell Media*

Mark F. Kendall
*General Manager
YBP Library Services*

Elisabeth Leonard, MSLS, MBA
SAGE Publishing

Jayne Marks
*Vice President, Global Publishing
Wolters Kluwer Health Learning,
Research & Practice*

Alison Mudditt
*Director
University of California Press*

Carol S. Richman

Rebecca Seger
*Senior Director of Institutional Sales
Oxford University Press*

Steven D. Smith, D.Phil.
John Wiley & Sons Inc

Stephen Rhind-Tutt
Alexander Street Press

Barbara Walthall
*Director of Publishing
American Political Science Association*

Jenni Wilson
*Sales Specialist, Ebooks
Proquest*

James Wiser
*Library Consortium Director
Community College League
of California*

About the Contributors

James Wiser, Library Consortium Director, Community College League of California, has almost 15 years in the library and publishing industry. James has worked seven years as a traditional librarian, five years as a library consortium officer, and two and a half years as an employee of a large academic publisher. He likes to joke that in any negotiation between a library, a consortium, or a publisher, he has at one time occupied each seat at that table.

In his current role as a library consortium director, James enjoys the variety of his every day. He says, "I love getting to know a little bit about so many different libraries but not enough that I see many of their challenges or need to take responsibility for those challenges. It's like being a grandparent, I think!" As he navigates in his current profession, James has a distinct leadership strategy. His three guiding values are transparency, authenticity, and example-setting. Honest communication, James feels, is an integral part of leading a team, and a team needs to know not just the decisions that have been made but the rationale behind them. Understanding that rationale helps coworkers to internalize the organization's values, which helps guide their work on a daily basis. James states, "I believe good leaders also need to be authentic: there's no one, single way to be a good leader, but your leadership style needs to come from who you truly are as a human being or people will not take you seriously. I try to model what I would most like to see in those I lead; most people can sniff out hypocrisy fairly easily." Professionally, James is inspired by the ability to make progress on needed change. James explains, "I heard someone once say that some great leaders are philosophers and other great leaders are plumbers. Admittedly, I'm more of a plumber; I like to roll up my sleeves and get things done. Lots of meandering, conversational indecision frustrates me more than anything else, and I don't like posturing or strategizing that does not directly impact real-world situations."

If he moved into a position within an academic library, the job James would most want would be that of a Scholarly Communications librarian. He says, "I think with my experience with libraries, publishers, and licensing, a role like that would play to my natural strengths and interests." When asked what he would like to do if he left the library or publishing world entirely, James imagines it would be fun to manage a luxury resort. Ideally in Hawaii.

Rolf A. Janke, founder of Mission Bell Media, has spent 37 years in higher education publishing. When Rolf joined Blackwell Publishers more than two decades ago, he worked in the college textbook side of the business, but quickly understood the significant role academic libraries play in the campus community. After attending his first American Library Association (ALA) conference, Rolf remembers being amazed how large the industry was and has remained on the library publishing side ever since. His favorite parts of his job are the external-facing components, such as talking to prospective authors, meeting librarians in their workspace, or talking to vendors and getting their perspective on the library business. Rolf enjoys connecting with people in and around the library world. He says, "There's a lot to take in but it is satisfying trying to stay in the center of it all." When discussing leadership strategy, Rolf's advice is "To put yourself in everyone else's shoes. People respond when they realize you care about their situation, no matter how big or small it might be. Integrity always trumps greed or ignorance." Rolf also encourages going beyond an open door policy. "A good leader doesn't wait for staff to come to them, they are already out interacting with their team . . . leading them!"

When asked, "If tomorrow you moved into a position within an academic library, what job would you want?" Rolf answers easily, "It would have to be a reference librarian. I have met so many reference librarians and have so much respect for them. I would embrace and appreciate the challenges of what they have experienced over the years as technology, economics, and user experiences have changed so dramatically. I would also call up my favorite reference publishers, sit them down in a room, and ask "Where are we going from here?" In his current role as a publisher, Rolf is professionally inspired by the process of turning an idea, a discussion, or a lightbulb moment into a book. Through the process of actually making that book, Rolf finds inspiration in those he works with—creative and innovative people who are passionate about what they do. If Rolf weren't working in the publishing industry, he imagines an alternative career making wine. "Much like a book starting with a single idea, wine starts with a single grape, and a few years later, with a lot of luck, care, skill, and patience you create something that others will enjoy. There is something very romantic about that and I think it would be a very interesting adventure, much like the making of a book."

Robert W. Boissy, Director of Institutional Marketing and Account Development for Springer Nature, has been in the publishing business for 13 years. Prior to publishing, Robert worked for a subscription agent for 15 years. When asked how he found his way into the academic library landscape, Robert said, "I have a master's degree in library science as well as a Certificate of Advanced Study in Information Transfer, and always knew I wanted to be working in and around the academic library community. Building knowledge from knowledge never grows old." Robert likes the idea of helping librarians who have dedicated their lives to helping others with their information needs. If Robert weren't doing what he is doing now, he replies enthusiastically, "I would be working in an academic library, of course! Ideally, as an Assessment librarian, with some Reference and Bibliographic Instruction duty. I would like to tell the story of the library in a way that no administrator could doubt its value."

Michael Levine-Clark, Dean and Director of the University of Denver Libraries, has worked in libraries for over 20 years. Initially, Michael found his way into the library landscape simply as a way to make money. He says, "I worked in bookstores during and after college and couldn't see a sustainable career, so I decided to go to library school." Michael says that his favorite part of working at a university is that he is surrounded by smart people doing interesting things, allowing him to continually learn. For most of his career, he's been a Collection Development librarian, responsible for providing the resources that support teaching and research. He loves the fact that his acquisitions choices have helped to shape a collection that will serve students and faculty long into the future. If he had to switch careers, Michael feels that he might explore publishing, which was the other career path he considered, but is thankful that "libraries are here to stay!"

Mark Kendall, General Manager, YBP Library Services, has been in publishing for 32 years—20 of which he worked with a library book/service provider. Mark enjoys the fact that no two days at his job are ever the same. He feels this variety "creates an environment of continuous energy, occasional angst, and plenty of excitement." He continues, "As a service provider, we are constantly evaluating, and reevaluating, how we can best meet our customer's evolving needs in an increasingly digital world. In the fast-paced ecosystem in which we work, embracing ambiguity while continually innovating are the most enjoyable parts of my work." Mark's leadership strategy is to lead by example and hire, develop, and support the best people in the industry, with a preference for those who demonstrate vision. He finds inspiration in the feeling that he is an active participant in delivering content that supports global education and helps develop and shape the leaders of tomorrow. When asked what he would do if he weren't in his current role, he answers, "I suspect I would be working somewhere within the publishing or education field or, perhaps more likely, running a bed-and-breakfast inn somewhere in New England."

Elisabeth Leonard has spent more than five years in publishing. Elisabeth became an academic librarian in 1997 because she found the process of research and helping others get the information they need both enjoyable and satisfying. When asked about her leadership strategy, Elisabeth says, "Supportive innovation has been my mantra throughout my career. When there is a problem, the staff most impacted should resolve the issue in a way that best fits the organizational culture and vision—striving for excellence but unimpaired by the notion of failure." She believes that a leader should be present to provide vision and the support to experiment. Elisabeth finds professional inspiration in talking to researchers at all levels. She states, "Whether talking to an undergraduate student or a seasoned researcher, hearing about their passion for resolving research questions and making research findings available in some form is motivational." When questioned about what position she would want if working in an academic library, she has trouble coming up with an answer because she has loved every library job she had—reference librarian, head of reference, and associate dean. She adds, "I think if I went back into higher education, I'd like to teach library science. I have had a lot of varied experience and think it would help inform future librarians."

Jayne Marks, Vice President Global Publishing for Health Learning, Research & Practice at Wolters Kluwer, has been working in publishing for 35 years. Jayne was always fascinated by science but realized during her time at college that bench research was not right for her. Working on scientific publications seemed the next best thing and she has been doing that ever since. Jayne's leadership strategy is to be clear about where you need to go as a team, give support and guidance where needed, and then get out of the way and let them succeed. She says, "Always be prepared to listen and never stop giving feedback." Professionally, Jayne says there is nothing more inspiring than hearing from a nurse or resident that one of their products has helped them do a better job. When asked if she moved into a position within an academic library tomorrow, which job she would want, Jayne muses, "I'd probably want to teach students how to find and value good quality, trusted content. I'm not sure that is a full-time job so I would probably want to work on building the library websites so that students could find what they are looking for." Or, as a backup, she jokes that she would probably try her hand at professional golf!

Alison Mudditt, Director, University of California (UC) Press, has spent 28 years in publishing. Alison finds the most rewarding part of her job is the time she gets to spend on campuses talking with librarians, faculty, students, and university leaders. She feels that relationship building is critical for her to understand the needs and challenges of library patrons and in doing so she is able to connect with their needs in a very real way. Alison says, "One achievement I'm really proud of over the past five years at UC Press has been the close relationship we have built with our libraries through the California Digital Library, the team of university librarians, and the awesome staff across the UC Libraries. They have been an incredible source of ideas, feedback, and support." When asked where she finds her professional inspiration, Alison answers with excitement, "I'm inspired and motived by the incredible scholarship that we publish and the opportunities provided by new technologies, not only to democratize access to this content but to help us make more efficient and effective use of our accumulating knowledge." Motivated by the mission to add reach and impact to this scholarship, Alison hopes that the work published at UC Press can deepen understanding and drive progressive change. "When I hear our authors interviewed as experts in national and global media on the Flint water crisis, the pursuit of war criminals, the unequal impact of economic hard times on women, or the immigration crisis in the Sonoran Desert, I feel deeply proud of the work we do."

Rebecca Seger, Senior Director of Institutional Sales, Oxford University Press, has 29 years in publishing. Rebecca relates that her career path started "Long ago and far away." At the age of 16, Rebecca had a summer job working for Combined Book Exhibit, a publishing service company that attended conferences displaying books for thousands of publishers. As a voracious reader growing up, Rebecca immediately felt at home. She states, "While I have had a variety of jobs in publishing, working with libraries always felt like what I was meant to do." Rebecca attended her first American Library Association conference at 18, after her freshman year of college. To this day, Rebecca's favorite part of her job is attending conferences and meeting with librarians from around the world. She values working with amazing people based in New York but also in Oxford UP offices around the world. When asked about her leadership strategy, Rebecca says, "Authenticity is key to my leadership strategy. Open communication, clear visibility of goals, and motivating my team to feel like they are part of something meaningful are all keys to how I lead my team." When asked to imagine a career in the library, Rebecca feels that she would enjoy a position as the head of collection development, saying, "I would know how to negotiate with publishers and vendors!" If she wasn't working in publishing, Rebecca imagines she would be working in her husband's family business, a service organization serving the community she lives in and the surrounding area

Dr. Steven D. Smith, John Wiley & Sons Inc., has 25 years in publishing. Steven fell into publishing by accident but quickly found that he enjoyed formulating and implementing strategy in the junction of corporate objectives and culture. Professionally, Steven finds challenge not only in correctly identifying strategic threats and opportunities but in seeking input, counsel, and advice. As a leader, Steven is deeply committed to a collaborative style of leadership. He says, "My time at Blackwell and Wiley has helped me to promote ideas, knowledge, discovery, and learning in ways that enable students, teachers, and researchers to succeed. These deeply held values have sustained us in our mission, whether in good times or when we have faced uncertainty and turbulent change." If he had not followed his heart into the publishing world, Steven can imagine himself making the transition to being a fiction writer or a painter. But, he says, "I'm an entrepreneur at heart. What I have in mind is a business at the intersection of digital archiving, strategy, and publishing," and he adds with a wink, "if someone would like to get involved, please do get in touch!"

Stephen Rhind-Tutt, President of Alexander Street Press, has worked in publishing for almost 30 years. Stephen found his way into the academic library landscape after he was recruited in 1987 by a fledgling CD-ROM publisher, Abt Books. From there he was hired to run the Health Science publishing division of SilverPlatter Information, one of the first and largest vendors of CD-ROM. "It was a great experience and hugely fun." said Stephen. "At that time library after library was experimenting with their very first electronic products." Stephen then moved to head up product management for Information Access Company, now a part of Gale/Cengage. He then moved to head up Chadwyck-Healey (U.S.), which was moving online from being a CD-ROM publisher. In 2000, when Chadwyck-Healey was acquired by ProQuest, Stephen cofounded Alexander Street Press. He grew it to a staff of more than 100 and some 150 products before selling it in June 2016 to ProQuest. During his career Stephen has been involved in many innovations, including one of the first electronic journal publications, the first streaming services for libraries, the first database of comics for libraries, and much more. During his career he has managed nearly 500 electronic library products.

Carol S. Richman is a veteran of the publishing industry. When asked about the favorite part of her job, Carol responds, "The favorite part of my job has been working with librarians and helping sales staff close deals." Professionally, Carol is inspired by knowing the landscape and learning more about how things change. If Carol suddenly changed careers and moved into a position within an academic library, she says she would want to work at the Help Desk and have the ability to work directly with library users either via e-mail or face-to-face.

Barbara Walthall, American Political Science Association, has been working in publishing for 34 years. Barbara unexpectedly found herself gravitating to publishing when she found that attention to detail, scheduling, communication, and books all found a home in publishing. Another way to look at it, she jokes, is that "It was a good field for someone slightly obsessive/compulsive to find success and fulfillment." She feels the best aspect of her job has been working directly with authors to prepare their manuscripts for publication. Barbara states, "I enjoy that collaboration and fulfillment in seeing something rough become polished and then published in a valuable form. Building that trust and communication can sometimes be a challenge, but is always worth the effort." She believes in being part of a team and embracing the different strengths each player brings to the team. Barbara believes that in publishing, the team includes the typesetter, the printer, the copyeditor, the managing editor, and the marketing staff. She states emphatically, "Everyone contributes to the success and everyone should be treated with the same respect." If she were not employed in her current position, Barbara would be tempted by many opportunities, but theater easily comes to mind. She says, ". . . maybe children's theater in underserved communities. There is great power in the arts."

Jenni Wilson, Sales Specialist for Ebooks at ProQuest, has been working in publishing and library sales for more than 20 years. The journey to sales began after finishing her master of library and information science (MLIS) degree at University of Illinois. After that, she headed down to Texas, where she worked as an assistant librarian in a two-person geology and petroleum engineering library (it was Houston, after all) and a bookstore. After leaving Texas and heading back to Illinois, Jenni found herself, for a number of reasons, looking for jobs outside a traditional library setting. Given her pre–library school background in sales and customer service, she started looking at positions being offered by publishers and other library vendors. According to Jenni, being in a sales position has many advantages, but the one that she enjoys the most is the experience of meeting people from around the country and around the world. When asked about what inspires her professionally, Jenni says, "I find inspiration in people who manage to be successful without being overly dramatic or overly challenging." When imagining a move to a position within an academic library, Jenni is intrigued by the task of managing electronic resources, acquisitions, and organization.

1

LIBRARIAN LEADERSHIP

Michael Levine-Clark

////////////// TOP TAKEAWAYS IN THIS CHAPTER

» Libraries and their users rely on publishers, so librarians need to understand publishing

» Librarians can benefit themselves, their institutions, and their profession by building relationships with publishers

» By serving on publishers' Library Advisory Boards (LABs), participating on joint library–publisher committees, and attending or speaking at publisher conferences, librarians can learn from and impact publishers

As an academic librarian, I have spent my career building library collections to support the university's mission. These collections comprise mostly books and journals that are produced and distributed by publishers. When libraries purchased physical books and maintained subscriptions to paper journals, it might have been possible to be an effective collections manager without understanding the publishing business, but that is clearly not the case in this era of digital resources. My job is to negotiate with publishers or third-party vendors about access terms and pricing for large bundles of content. I need to understand a range of different business models and choose the best one for a particular resource for my institution. It's impossible to do this without having a clear understanding of how publishing works, why publishers make the decisions they do, and how publishers run their businesses. Understanding can come from reading and studying the business, but often it also requires building personal relationships, attending conferences, and talking to publishers.

Librarians can better serve their institutions and the profession by working closely with publishers. This work can influence both the business models that publishers employ and the decisions that librarians make in working with publishers. My own leadership in working with publishers has been in three broad areas, each of which impacts the library–publisher relationship in different ways: (1) serving on publishers' library advisory boards (LABs), (2) serving on joint committees within professional organizations, and (3) attending and sometimes presenting at publisher-focused conferences. By taking advantage of opportunities to meet with publishers and building these important relationships, librarians can set up their institutions to benefit directly as I have. When librarians have research projects to complete (for the benefit of the profession or simply to help on the road toward tenure), publisher contacts can often provide data or insight that will improve the overall project. This is particularly true of projects about usage or discovery. Strong relationships can help librarians negotiate better deals, develop mutually beneficial best practices, and establish better library workflows.

Many librarians not only do not take the time to engage with publishers and build relationships, they are actively opposed to doing so. At a major library conference a few years ago, the librarian giving the opening plenary spent a lot of time talking about her difficult relationships with vendors. She characterized the library–vendor relationship as abusive and shared stories about bad experiences with various publishers. During the question-and-answer session at the end of her talk, one of these publishers offered to discuss their differences over coffee, an offer the speaker refused. Her refusal to even talk to a publisher has stuck with me as being particularly shortsighted. Yet, while many of the librarians in the audience were turned off by her talk, it was clear from comments, applause, and the social media reaction afterward that many librarians felt empowered by her remarks. Most librarians who negotiate with publishers have been frustrated at one time or another by license terms or pricing or even a particular sales person. Those of us who manage collections budgets have experienced the frustration of watching inflation of our journal packages outpace our funding levels. But, for me, the response to this frustration has always been to talk *more* with publishers, not to shut them out.

Libraries rely on the content that publishers produce. More importantly, our users rely on that content. We need the books and journals that publishers provide because they are the resources our users expect. We're ultimately here to serve our students and faculty, and until they tell us otherwise, we should continue to acquire the publisher-generated content they want. Given our need for publishers, refusing to speak to them is doing a disservice to our users. We need to engage with publishers so we can understand how and why they make the decisions they do. This engagement helps us build collections our users want and makes us better librarians.

Since early in my career I have devoted a lot of effort to getting to know publishers. I've taken the time to get to know them as colleagues and have shared many cups of coffee with them (and other beverages). In so doing, I am sure that I have saved my university much more money than the plenary speaker saved hers by walking away and refusing to have coffee with a publisher. I've also learned a lot about the publishing business, knowledge that I think has helped me as a negotiator and an advocate for libraries.

There are many opportunities for librarians to lead the profession by working with publishers. Most of the larger academic publishers have library advisory boards (LABs) where librarians can provide advice, learn about new and forthcoming developments, and hopefully influence publishers to adopt mutually beneficial sales and access models. Librarians can also join committees of organizations such as the National Information Standards Organization (NISO)[1] that include stakeholders from across the entire scholarly communications ecosystem, from libraries to publishers to vendors, or join committees of publisher-focused organizations such as the Society for Scholarly Publishing (SSP).[2] In either case, professional service can foster collaboration and understanding and can lead to improved outcomes for libraries. Perhaps easier than joining a committee or getting invited to join a LAB, librarians should pay attention to the schedule of publisher conferences and attend sessions at the Association of American University Presses (AAUP)[3] or Association of Learned & Professional Society Publishers (ALPSP).[4] I try to attend as many of these conferences as possible, and by attending sessions I learn more about how the publishing business works. In some cases I have spoken at these publisher-oriented conferences, giving me a stage to directly convey a librarian's perspective to a large audience of publishers.

Library Advisory Boards (LABs)

Perhaps because I have clearly valued building relationships with publishers, I have been asked to serve on quite a few publishers' library advisory boards and currently serve on eight publisher boards plus two publisher services boards. That is a lot of boards—many would say I devote too much time to this—but I know I personally benefit from what I learn and I think my university benefits as well.

Serving on publisher advisory boards, and offering informal advice to publishers at other times, is valuable in multiple ways. On the most basic level, I like knowing how publishing works. More importantly, what I learn can help me negotiate with publishers. But I am also able to play an advocacy role, giving publishers advice about pricing models, user experience, and library needs, hopefully benefiting libraries and end users everywhere.

In one recent publisher LAB meeting, my colleagues and I were given an opportunity to provide advice about how two journal publishers that had recently merged could integrate sales models and title lists in a way that would allow libraries to transition to a single package. We were presented with detailed information about why the merger occurred, what the new combined publisher hoped to accomplish, and some of the very specific challenges they faced in terms of workplace culture and integrating two very different models for selling journal packages.

They showed us several proposed models and then asked us to provide feedback. We talked about what we felt the market would bear, how we would react in our specific libraries, what we felt was possible in terms of budget, and some of our frustrations in managing large journal packages. When the publisher introduced the final model, it was not ideal, but it also showed clear evidence that some of our suggestions had been incorporated. In this case the library leaders on this LAB were able to help shift a sales model in a way that would benefit libraries more than the initial models the publisher was considering.

Several years ago another publisher introduced comprehensive e-book packages but without the ability to sell any titles individually. When they presented this model to the LAB, we responded that it was crucial for us to be able to purchase individual titles, whether as part of an approval plan or as direct orders. Unfortunately, they had been so sure that packages were the right approach that they had not designed their system to allow title-by-title sales, so it was not a model they could easily switch away from. After two years of discussion with the LAB, including some of us giving presentations about how we managed our monograph acquisitions workflow, this publisher invested in developing a new system that allowed title-by-title sales. This was a clear success and an example of library leaders on the LAB directly and positively influencing change in a way that benefited all libraries.

Sometimes participation on a LAB can lead to opportunities to pilot new projects or programs. Through discussions about e-book models at different LABs, I was able to work with one publisher to pilot a range of different pricing structures for different subject packages on their platform. We purchased a few packages based on the list price with a standard discount; some others based on historical purchase patterns (with a discount off the list price, based on the percentage of titles from that publisher that we normally purchased in that subject area); others based on historical usage patterns (with a discount based on the percentage of titles from that publisher that were normally used); and some others that we turned on and agreed to purchase based on the actual usage rate (an early version of evidence-based selection). We did this for a year, allowing both my library and the publisher to learn about demand for e-books and allowing the publisher to pilot sales models. Usage was good and we ultimately ended up negotiating a license for all of this publisher's e-books, with a nice discount. While this was only a pilot, we were able to learn more about e-book use, something that benefited both parties and helped the publisher learn more about how to sell e-book packages to libraries.

Another example of a project arising out of a LAB involves another librarian who worked with a large STM publisher (STM is a global trade association for academic and professional publishers) to harvest publisher metadata and open access versions of articles to populate her institutional repository. She reported on this project at the LAB meeting and now we are discussing a pilot to expand it to include additional publishers and libraries. While that has not happened yet, both the large and small projects are examples of library leaders leveraging partnerships with publishers to increase efficiencies by automating a labor-intensive process. If this pilot expands to become a standard workflow, it will save staff time in many libraries.

Joint Committees

In most cases, librarians who volunteer to serve in professional organizations end up serving exclusively with other librarians. Most library associations, as one would expect, are made up mostly of librarians, so committee work tends to focus on library issues. Similarly, most publishers end up focusing on issues that are specific to publishing. But there are joint committees either within library- or publisher-focused associations or within organizations that are explicitly designed to involve the full range of stakeholders. As a library leader, I have benefited from serving on one such committee and will seek out similar opportunities. The National Information Standards Organization (NISO) is a perfect example of an organization that brings librarians and publishers together. With a mandate to include all stakeholders in the process of developing standards or best practices, NISO always includes a mix of librarians, publishers, and other information professionals on its committees. Several years ago I cochaired the NISO Demand-Driven Acquisitions (DDA) for Monographs Working Group, which wrote a recommended practice document for DDA.[5] Our committee included leaders from the library, publishing, and vendor communities and had to come up with a recommended practice that would work for each of these groups.

As the NISO DDA Working Group explored best practices, it became quite clear that publishers were very concerned about the impact that DDA broadly and short-term loans (STLs) specifically were having on sales of monographs. We warned that "Publishers reporting decreased revenue are questioning whether STLs have contributed to that trend. . . . It is important to acknowledge the reality that there may be loss of revenue and that loss of revenue may negatively impact publishers' ability to publish books and support the scholarly ecosystem. We must establish STL models that take into account this financial reality or STL as a model will not be sustainable at all."[6] Not long after this, publishers did in fact raise the cost of STLs, and many librarians reacted with surprise and outrage.[7] My own understanding of monographic publishing costs and publisher expectations around sales, as well as the specific conversations we had within the NISO DDA Working Group, made it clear that the STL model then in place would have to change.

While I have not served on other NISO committees, I know from talking to other librarians that they too learn a great deal from publishers while serving on these committees and are also able to educate publishers about specific library needs and concerns.

There are chances to serve on committees within library organizations that include publishers and within publisher organizations that include librarians. For example, the Publisher-Vendor-Library Relations (PVLR) Interest Group within the Association for Library Collections and Technical Services (ALCTS) has library, publisher, and vendor representatives who together plan programs that are held during American Library Association (ALA) conferences and that focus on current topics that impact librarians, publishers, and vendors.[8] On the publisher side, the Society for Scholarly Publishing (SSP) usually has a few librarians serving on committees.[9]

By serving together with publishers on committees that help advance common interests, librarians can both learn from and inform publishers about library concerns. This is an excellent way for a librarian to broaden his or her skills and lead the profession in a positive way.

Publisher-Focused Conferences

Over the years I have had the opportunity to speak at several publisher conferences. Speaking directly to publishers, societies, and editors, most of whom do not regularly interact with librarians, has given me a chance to educate them about library trends and to learn from them as well. I have always taken the opportunity to attend as many sessions at these conferences as possible, so I come away learning more about how publishers work—some of this is simply informative (such as learning about the various publisher services companies) and some is useful in thinking about library–publisher interactions (such as an early panel discussion about JSTOR [a digital library founded in 1995] and Project Muse e-books at an annual meeting of the Association of American University Presses).

I have spoken at AAUP conferences several times: on DDA, on library e-book preferences, and on open access models for monographs. In each case, I was able to insert a library perspective into a publisher-centered discussion. In 2010, when DDA was just beginning to emerge in a significant way in North American academic libraries, I participated in a panel, "Rethinking Library Acquisition: Demand-Driven Purchasing for Scholarly Books," that was clearly—from the questions and comments—the first exposure to this important new concept for many in the audience. In 2011, I gave a presentation, "E-Book Aggregators: What Do Libraries Want?" as part of a program on "Selling to Libraries: The New E-Book Aggregation Options." I stressed the importance of fitting into existing library workflows, needing to be able to purchase title-by-title, and working with multiple aggregators. At this session, too, it was clear to me that some of the publishers in the room had not thought about these issues: for instance, some were planning to sell via only one aggregator. In my experiences speaking at AAUP conferences, I have come away feeling that I made a difference in how publishers decided to work with libraries.

Another worthwhile experience has been to participate in the SSP Librarian Focus Group, a day-long panel in which four or five librarians sit in front of a room full of scholarly publishers and editors for a day, answering questions on a broad range of topics.[10] I have done this twice and hope to have the opportunity to do so again. The audience is mostly smaller society publishers who do not regularly talk to librarians, so it is an excellent opportunity to educate publishers about library trends and concerns.

I have spoken about open access at the 2015 AAUP Annual Meeting and at the 2016 Council of Science Editors Annual Meeting. In both cases I was there to give a librarian's perspective to a room full of people making decisions about open access publishing that could impact libraries directly. In June 2016, I participated in a daylong seminar, "The Publisher's and Librarian's Challenge: Models, Practices, and Products to Sustain OA Publishing," sponsored by ALPSP. This session was likely to have some librarians in the audience, but most of the attendees were publishers. As we consider an open future, it is crucial that librarians understand publisher decisions and that publishers understand library needs. Librarians who can navigate both worlds have the opportunity to provide a crucial leadership role.

Speaking to groups of publishers at conferences has been valuable to me as a means of influencing decisions about access models that directly impact library workflow and acquisitions options. While I do not believe that my voice alone would sway a publisher's overall strategy, I do hope that I have been able to influence them in a small way on behalf of all libraries.

Taking Advantage of Publisher Relations

While there is inherent value in learning more about publishers, teaching them about libraries, and influencing them in a small way, I have also experienced tangible benefits in terms of my research. In one specific example, I conducted a study with two librarian colleagues about the impact of discovery system implementation on the usage of publisher-hosted journals.[11] To conduct this study, we examined usage of journals from six different publishers at 33 different libraries before and after they implemented a discovery system. My coauthors and I are all on multiple LABs and have built deep relationships with publishers. We were able to use those connections to get publishers to share usage data with us (with the explicit permission of the libraries involved), something that would have been difficult without those connections.

I also do a lot of work looking at usage of library collections. I have frequently turned to publishers to obtain data beyond the basic COUNTER (Counting Online Usage of Networked Electronic Resources) reports they are required to supply. Being able to access more nuanced data has made it possible for me to conduct better research and has sometimes impacted collection development decisions in my library as well.

Conclusion

While some librarians seem to view the librarian–publisher relationship as adversarial, and even actively avoid building relationships, I believe that it is in both of our best interests to strengthen those relationships as much as possible. In my own experience, I have served on LABs, worked with publishers on committees, and spoken at publisher conferences. In each of these cases, I have influenced (even if only in a small way) publisher decisions that impacted libraries. I have been able to establish pilot projects that benefited my library while also helping a publisher partner, and have used publisher connections to help with my research. I have also learned a great deal from publishers. This knowledge makes me a better librarian and ultimately helps me serve my institution better.

Librarians who are interested in leading the profession can make a difference by cultivating relationships with publishers and by translating between the two groups. By serving together on committees, by participating on LABs, and by attending or speaking at publisher-focused conferences, librarians will understand a key stakeholder in the scholarly information ecosystem that is so valuable to all of us.

The Future

>> As we move toward open access and other new models of publishing, librarians have the opportunity to impact publishers in important ways
>> Librarians need to work with publishers to ensure that scholarly publishing continues to thrive
>> Librarians can work with publishers to develop innovative solutions to problems that haven't even been imagined yet

Notes

1. National Information Standards Organization (NISO), http://www.niso.org/home (Accessed May 2016).

2. Society for Scholarly Publishing (SSP), https://www.sspnet.org (Accessed May 2016).

3. Association of American University Presses (AAUP), http://www.aaupnet.org (Accessed May 2016).

4. Association of Learned and Professional Society Publishers (ALPSP), http://www.alpsp.org (Accessed May 2016).

5. "Demand Driven Acquisition of Monographs: A Recommended Practice of the National Information Standards Organization." http://www.niso.org/apps/group_public/download.php /13373/rp-20-2014_DDA.pdf (Accessed May 2016).

6. "Demand Driven Acquisition of Monographs: A Recommended Practice of the National Information Standards Organization." p. 6. http://www.niso.org/publications/rp http://www.niso.org /apps/group_public/download.php/13373/rp-20-2014_DDA.pdf (Accessed May 2016).

7. Wolfman-Arent, Avi. "College Libraries Push Back as Publishers Raise Some E-Book Prices." *Chronicle of Higher Education*, June 16, 2014. http://chronicle.com/article/College-Libraries-Push -Back-as/147085 (Accessed May 2016).

8. Publisher-Vendor-Library Relations Interest Group (PVLR). http://www.ala.org/alcts/mgrps /ig/ats-pvlr (Accessed May 2016).

9. SSP Committees. http://www.resourcenter.net/Scripts/4Disapi2.dll/4DCGI/committees /Listing2.html?Action=List_Committees (Accessed May 2016).

10. Society for Scholarly Publishing, Librarian Focus Groups. https://www.sspnet.org/events /librarian-focus-groups (Accessed May 2016).

11. Levine-Clark, Michael, John McDonald, and Jason Price. "Discovery or Displacement? A Large-Scale Longitudinal Study of the Effect of Discovery Systems on Online Journal Usage." *Insights*, v.27/3 (2014): 249–256.

2

DYSTOPIA OR UTOPIA? THE ROLE OF THE 21ST-CENTURY COMMERCIAL PUBLISHER

Stephen Rhind-Tutt

Once upon a time . . .

Once upon a time it was simple. If you'd written something good, you'd get published. Many thousands of publishers produced nicely defined packages known as books, magazines, journals, newspapers, and similar products that were sold through lots of physical outlets and via the mail. They were selected and curated by editors, experts in their fields who helped shape the content. Even the most frequent publications came out no more than once a day, and most publishing cycles were measured in months. Books, films, and music, by and large, had independent creation and distribution networks. Everyone knew their roles and generally competed within boundaries. Journalists had time to research and write great pieces. Readers knew where to go to get the best content—their favorite bookshops and their favorite sections in libraries.

Academic publishing sat neatly within this ecosystem. Faculty knew which journals to publish in and the value of publishers was evident to all. Prices were straightforward and, by and large, regarded as fair. Collection development librarians sorted through thousands of works from hundreds of publishers on behalf of faculty, diligently choosing the best content to buy and preserve for posterity. Catalogers worked hard to categorize and ensure that these works were discoverable. Publishers, universities, and their libraries contributed to the creation of scholarship in a seemingly well-balanced way.

We all know how it is now.

Many of those involved in this ecosystem feel themselves to be under threat. Publishers feel threatened by authors who publish directly to their readers. Smaller publishers feel threatened by larger companies that control distribution. Larger publishers feel threatened by open access and an increasingly active customer base that resents their hegemony. Librarians feel threatened by disintermediation as faculty get content directly from the web and from publishers who charge too much. Even the university itself is under threat as online courses and companies like Udemy and Coursera grow ever more effective in automated online education. These fears are endlessly debated in library- and publisher-oriented publications and on the websphere. Incumbents staunchly defend their role in the ecosystem but, at the same time, suggest that others will have to change quickly or lose their place within it.

Many suggest that the demise and change within their areas will have dire consequences for learning, scholarship, and society as a whole, and argue that the value they bring to the party is undervalued and misunderstood. In academic publishing this debate has publishers defending the value of peer review, editorial selection, and the costs of maintaining high-quality platforms. Universities ask why they're paying to access information that they themselves created and why prices are increasing when the costs to produce content are declining. Students (or the parents of students) ask why education has become so expensive, even as new technologies make it easier to teach.

The alternative view is precisely the opposite. Authors, readers, students, and teachers have never had it so good. More quality content is available for less money to more people than ever before. Via cell phones, literally billions of people can learn faster, more easily, and with more functionality than at any point in history. The technologies that made this possible continue to improve, get cheaper, and grow in acceptance. It's not unrealistic to believe that, say in 20 years, 70 percent of the world will have access to automated tools that will give them a better basic education than most receive today. Having set the landscape, I'd now like to work through the following questions:

>> What kind of organization is a 21st-century publishing company?

>> What kind of skills are required from individuals publishing in the 21st century?

>> What kind of challenges and opportunities are such companies and individuals facing?

The 21st-Century Publishing Company

The *Oxford English Dictionary* defines a publisher as "A company or person that prepares and issues books, journals, or music for sale." Far too narrow a description in my opinion. Too narrow in its definition of content—what about software publishers, database publishers, software gaming companies, app creators, news services, blogs, archives, and videos? Too narrow in its definition of organizations—what about societies, libraries, open access advocates, think tanks, and even presidential campaigns? Too narrow in its definition of role—what about video producers, bloggers, librarians, catalogers, peer reviewers, and writers of reviews? My definition would be much broader: An organization or person that creates or adds value to content. I've had this view for a long time and see a lot of pushback from traditional publishers claiming it's far too broad. But if you look not at organizational roles but at what is produced, then I think it's self-evident. Ask yourself what are the canonical publications of our time—the publications that people will refer to in 100 years? Some 30 years ago that list of "must-have titles for libraries" included *Encyclopedia Britannica*, Facts on File, and Books In Print. There was common agreement that these were essential resources for every academic library. Today those publications are supplanted by Wikipedia, Google, and Amazon—arguably the largest, most consulted, and most important reference works. You may not think of them as publications, but the truth is they do exactly what the earlier titles did and the organizations that create them are, by my definition, publishers.

Wikipedia is easy to view in this regard. It used the seminal 1911 edition of *Encyclopedia Britannica* as the basis for some of its early articles. Its mission is "to empower and engage people around the world to collect and develop educational content under a free license or in the public domain, and to disseminate it effectively and globally." Wikipedia uses human editors to write, edit, and improve articles written by authors, just as a traditional publisher does. Since its launch it has become more and more like a traditional publisher, with its editors conforming to well-established editorial policies. At the same time, traditional publishers have moved closer and closer to Wikipedia, as they let their readers annotate, comment, and suggest improvements to existing works. There is little doubt in my mind that the 5.1 million articles the site offers, the billions who have and will read it, and the millions who've contributed to it, make Wikipedia the most important publication of our day.

It's less clear that Google is a publisher. Its techno-centricity, advertising-based business model, and the fact that it appears not to commission content seem to disqualify it. But look again and you'll see it's engaged in the same process that publishers (and for that matter librarians) have for the last century. A clue is found in its mission "to organize the world's information and make it universally accessible and useful" (i.e., the same mission as many libraries and publishers). It seeks out great content and presents it to its readers. It makes more use of human labor than any publisher does—just in a different way. Human input is the basis for the algorithm that Google uses to select what to disseminate. It even commissions content directly from (video) producers and pays substantial royalties to (video) authors. The difference between it and a traditional publisher is in method, not purpose.

Even Amazon should be considered a publisher—and not just for its efforts to commission and license original authors and content. Its mission is to "to be Earth's most customer-centric company for four primary customer sets: consumers, sellers, enterprises, and content creators." That doesn't sound much like a traditional publisher, but poke a little deeper and it's clear it is. It wants to secure the best content possible, add value where it can, make the content it publishes better cataloged, indexed, annotated, and interlinked, and shape content to be more effective on its devices. All of these are attributes of a 21st-century publisher.

The more one looks at the titans of the Internet, the more overlap one sees between their missions and those of publishers and libraries. Twitter, for example: "Our mission: To give everyone the power to create and share ideas and information instantly, without barriers." Facebook: "To give people the power to share and make the world more open and connected." LinkedIn: "To connect the world's professionals to make them more productive and successful." All of these companies see themselves as helping the creators of content (we used to call them authors) disseminate their ideas and content to consumers (we used to call them readers).

And this is just the present day. Technology will continue to improve. Some of the smartest minds in the world are actively pondering how better to improve publications, to lower the cost of peer review, and to establish systems that will automate historically labor-intensive processes like writing and even thinking. The tools that today help traditional editors commission, evaluate, correct, and improve manuscripts will themselves continue the long evolution they've been experiencing for so many years. Spell-checking, fact-checking, auto-correction, automated indexing, and automatic abstract generation are just the start of a long chain of improvements.

Some publishers argue that the distinction between what they offer and what is offered by these other companies is the quality of the information they provide, that it's peer-reviewed or vetted by humans. They maintain that this is the critical element that defines publishing and that there's something lost in automation that can never be replicated.

I'd counter that whether it's more reliable does not make Wikipedia any less of a publication, and that whether human input is used directly or via automated systems doesn't make Google any less of a publisher. Even with this distinction, the lines between traditional publishers and software companies are becoming more and more blurred. Traditional publishers are heavily adopting the techniques and tools the large Internet companies have created. Elsevier acquired the social network Mendeley. Most publishers are using algorithms to present more relevant content to users, leveraging their reading behavior. I suspect you, like me, enjoy and appreciate the crowd-sourced commentary and annotations alongside the pieces in the *Scholarly Kitchen*, the well-known blog from the Society of Scholarly Publishers.

Whenever a new technology makes an older one obsolete, there are champions for the old. It happened for vinyl records, steamship packages across the Atlantic, and railway journeys across the United States. Enthusiasts perpetuate and continue the old, but inevitably the new technology becomes the standard for the future. Yes, something is lost with machine-made shoes rather than a pair that's handmade, and something is lost when the creation, discovery, and consumption of books and journals moves to the Internet, but in most cases, publication is not a goal in and of itself. The academic publisher of the 21st century should be measured by whether it enables people to learn and teach cheaper, better, and faster, and facilitates discovery or advances scholarship. The excellence of a publisher is in its content and the value it adds, not the manner in which it adds the value.

What Skills Does a 21st-Century Publisher Need?

This move from the traditional print publisher to the 21st-century publisher is measured in years—some would argue decades. ERIC, NTIS, and MED-LINE—the first electronic databases aimed at scholarship and librarians—were launched some 50 years ago. Google is nearing its 20th birthday. The change may seem revolutionary, but it takes time, so those who wish to be publishers today need to be fluent both in new technologies as well as the old way of doing things. This makes for a long list of skills and capabilities.

When hiring for publishers today I look for the following:

» Creativity and an earnest wish to improve teaching and research
» An understanding of how scholarship and learning works
» Marketing and writing skills—an ability to articulate thoughts and ideas succinctly
» Discipline knowledge—an in-depth knowledge of a particular area
» Commissioning skills—an ability to persuade others to create high-quality content
» Licensing skills—the ability to persuade owners of copyright to license their content
» Legal skills—an ability to understand contracts and copyright law
» Technical understanding—knowledge of the new technology and the potential it has to offer, where the technology is heading, and what elements of technology are easy and which are hard

» Operations and process understanding—the ability to analyze work-flows, see where inefficiencies lie, and come up with new systems and processes to increase efficiency
» Business expertise—an ability to analyze usage, sales, and costs
» Management expertise—the ability to manage teams and lead across organizations

Finding someone with all of these skills is extremely difficult, almost impossible. So the challenge becomes management—how to assemble the varied parties and individuals who collectively deliver on this list. For most publishers the hard business and technical skills are the primary drivers of success, so naturally they tend to favor these items over the others. For me, the two most important ingredients are as follows:

» *A firm desire to improve teaching and/or research.* This can't be learned, and without it, an individual will not have the right motivation.
» *Business and management expertise.* Although this can be learned, many don't see or understand how important it is. Publications that aren't sustainable will fail. The challenge for the commercial publisher is not just to develop great scholarship and teaching tools, it's to do it profitably.

With these two skills, the rest can be developed.

Challenges and Opportunities

Let's take a look at the challenges and opportunities faced by publishers and publishing companies. The landscape publishers face today is not a forgiving one. Some trends appear inexorable:

Static/Declining Library Budgets

There are few new libraries being built in the developed world. Budgets for most libraries have been growing at rates below inflation. This means that overall spending in the library market is static. For publishers to grow, they need to displace competitors—by producing better and lower-priced products, by consolidation and cost efficiencies, or by finding new markets. This is why we see fewer and fewer companies in the library space and more and more efforts by publishers to move directly to faculty and to practitioners.

New Utility, Functionality, and Workflow

The ability of technology to enhance research and improve education has grown and will grow in leaps and bounds. Since around 2010, there have been significant advances in adaptive learning, mobile devices, data mining, data set publication, archive publications, workflow integration, automated testing, video creation, and video delivery—to name a few. Each of these enhancements must be paid for, usually by publishers investing and hoping to recoup that investment with sales. This, combined with reduced budgets, makes the environment extremely competitive. Publishers must invest, but at the same time they must find efficiencies, new markets, and new ways of doing this.

Consolidation

The very nature of the Internet favors consolidation. The network effects we see on Facebook apply equally to academic publishing. The ability for scholars to scan and read all content pertinent to a subject, to interact with all scholars with expertise on a subject, to analyze everything within a subject, and to participate in creating knowledge together—these are all forces that mean the larger a resource is, the more effective it's likely to be. The same applies to distribution. Amazon has an estimated share of 64 percent of online book sales.[1] Their market power enables them to pressure even the largest publishers for better margins, additional marketing spends, and standardized processes. Smaller publishers give them as much as a 60 percent discount. Today fewer than 10 percent of books are sold through independent bookstores. Fully 50 percent of independent bookstores have closed in the last 20 years. The same is true in the academic space. Seventy percent of journals in the social sciences are with the big five publishers.[2] In the 1970s that number was 20 percent.

Rise of Metrics

It is currently in vogue to measure success of a publication by how much it is used. This is a very broad approximation of whether an item is actually helping students learn or scholars discover. Improving learning or furthering discoveries are often inversely proportionate to use. The best system would involve having a person immediately find what they wanted in a document that conveys knowledge quickly. It would be used by many, but not for long. However, usage has the benefit of being easily understood and being somewhat comparable. It's the best system we've got and clearly an item that's never used never delivers value. There are many opportunities here to improve—which is why we see the rise of Altmetrics and similar tools to gauge research consumption.

ROI-Based Decision Making

Colleges and their libraries are under huge pressure to justify expenditures through ROI (return on investment) calculations based on usage. This should be welcome—it makes the allocation of resources more efficient. However, for research-oriented publishers, it presents problems, as the value delivered doesn't easily lend itself to that kind of calculation. This is particularly true of rare, archival content and monographs in fields that by their very nature are low use. The opportunity lies in developing comprehensive resources for particular disciplines where the value delivered is much larger than a simple article or monograph, and where the value is measured by how it has helped advance the scholarship and learning across the field.

How the 21st-Century Publisher Behaves

"Survival isn't mandatory," the late W. Edwards Deming is reputed to have said. Commercial academic publishing must make money in the new environment or it will quickly disappear. Dangers and opportunities in the marketplace must be anticipated, translated into strategies, made into plans, implemented, evaluated, and either discontinued or built further. New markets must be found, disappearing markets must be abandoned. A good businessperson has a broad array of tools at his or her disposal to effect change, but s/he must tread the balance between high risks and big opportunities. Their role is less to judge what's going on in the market and more to react to whatever is happening in the market in order to grow revenues and profits.

Growth, survival, and profits are driven by strategies so numerous I can't describe them here, but let's take a look at the most common ones:

» *Add value.* The opportunities to add value evolve over time. In years gone by publishers added value in matters like typesetting, printing, layout, warehousing, and distribution. As things have moved to digital, value is now added through increased functionality—items like mobile apps, the ability to search, and integration with third-party services like Blackboard or citation management systems. We can be sure that technology will continue to improve—this is a rich vein that's likely to continue.

» *Create and license the best content.* From finding the best authors to securing flagship journals from societies, publishers strive to secure the best content.

» *Protect existing revenues.* In this model the publisher aims to protect its current business as far as is possible. Journal publishers do this in all sorts of ways, for example, large advances, big-deal pricing, strict copyright enforcement, or hybrid open access for fee journals.

» *Become more efficient.* As the market changes, new opportunities emerge for efficiencies. Reducing inventory through print on demand, discontinuing unprofitable lines, and automating tasks that previously were done manually are all ways to increase efficiency.

» *Exit unprofitable businesses.* Recognize when you're in an indefensible position and react. For example, in the 1990s many microfilm publishers saw clearly that electronic publishing was going to render them uncompetitive and chose either to sell to a larger organization expert in that field (Primary Source Media) or to invest in new technology (University Microfilms International, now ProQuest).

» *Expand into new markets.* Electronic publishing makes it easier to reach international markets. The spread of English as the primary language of science lifts the interest in many new markets.

» *Economies of scale.* For example, the cost to maintain a system to produce and distribute journals is substantial. A publisher with thousands of journals can spread that cost widely, creating must-have packages that maximize revenues. A small, independent publisher with a few journals can find it very hard to compete. The same logic applies to consolidation; large vendors have hundreds of salespeople around the world.

» *Build on strengths.* Know which parts of your organization are competitively strong and build on them. Even though the primary focus of an organization may be publishing, it may license technology to third parties.

» *Be a first mover.* Project and anticipate what's going on in the landscape. Examine trends. Find opportunities and invest in them. For example, if you can see that tablets are going to become ubiquitous, be the first to have your content available in that format.

Most of these strategies are competitive rather than collaborative. Most publishers behave in Darwinian fashion. They fight aggressively with each other for a share of the market, especially when that market is declining.

A Dystopia?

I suspect there are many librarians who've read to this point who see the landscape I've painted and the one they experience as a dystopia. They see a 21st-century, metropolis-like vision in which humans are increasingly replaced by machines, or a world dominated by capitalists motivated by money and eager to perpetuate their monopolistic power. Here librarians and faculty are tied to systems and processes they disagree with and little hope for long-term change.

It is not true. In the long term, customers get what customers want. In some cases, like the early 19th-century railroads or oil monopolies, it took changes in legislation to force change, but no company survives the long term without giving its customers what they want. Today, large journal publishers may seem dominant, but they're benefiting because the Internet confers advantages of scale, especially when it comes to books and journals developed and delivered traditionally and because the academy continues to consider journals and books as the fundamental unit for delivering and consuming scholarly information. As long as academic credentialing bodies insist on traditional journal and monographic formats as the sole basis for scholarly expression and as long as faculty and credentialing committees insist on specific journals as the basis for publishing excellence, they have no motivation to change.

However, when confronted by new models like open access, publishers have already shown they'll adopt a different stance. They're investing in sites and services like Mendeley, ReadCube, FigShare, LabGuru, video, collaborative tools, open-access journals, blogs, and other academic websites. Publishers do this because they're following the strategies outlined above and because this is the way they can best increase their revenues and grow. They too are part of the system aiming to deliver scholarship and learning at lower cost. Many publishers have strong visions of how they can improve research and scholarship and, as the models that have served them well in the past become unprofitable, they will embrace the new.

Or Utopia?

I'm imagining a scholar writing 100 years from now. She's recording her thesis on the 21st-century publishing industry. Here's an extract:

In the early 21st century those charged with increasing knowledge and improving learning were still known as "publishers." The literature of that time shows that many felt that this was a dark time in which scholarship and learning were in retreat. However, we can now see that this was precisely the time when society truly discovered how to bring the benefits of scholarship and learning to large numbers of people. The cost per reader per article fell from several dollars to fractions of pennies. The speed with which information was disseminated went from days to milliseconds, the ability to collaborate around content remotely was invented, and ever more sophisticated tools allowed information to be mined, built upon, and turned into knowledge. Vast archives that had historically been inaccessible were made available online. By 2016, close to 40 percent[3] of the world's population had access to a free collaborative encyclopedia with more than 5.4 million articles. Every day nearly

3.5 billion searches were conducted across the leading search engine.[3] By 2050, 95 percent were able to rely on it for a basic education. This process was painful, but now, as we look back on it, we see it was inevitable. We only wish that those involved in the process had moved faster to adapt, because that in turn would have enabled humanity to benefit from it earlier.

The creation and consumption of information is part of a much larger process by which humans learn and discover. "Publishing" is just a part of the process—one step in the workflow of learning and research. There will be countless opportunities for individuals and organizations, even as technological developments pull us further and further away from our roots. Painful it may be, it's something that we should welcome.

Notes

1. Milliot, Jim. "Can Anyone Compete With Amazon?" *Publishers Weekly* (May 28, 2014).

2. Larivière, V., S. Haustein, and P. Mongeon. "The Oligopoly of Academic Publishers in the Digital Era." PLoS ONE 10(6): e0127502 (June 10, 2015). doi:10.1371/journal.pone.0127502 (Accessed October 2016).

3. Internet Live Stats. "Internet Users." www.internetlivestats.com/internet-users (Accessed October 2016).

—— 3 ——

UNIVERSITY PRESSES IN (PERMANENT) CRISIS: REINVENTING CULTURE AND COLLABORATION FOR THE DIGITAL AGE

Alison Mudditt

////////// **TOP TAKEAWAYS IN THIS CHAPTER**

» University presses play a crucial role in supporting scholarship that doesn't generate a market-based return

» Scholarly publishing—including monographic publishing—is labor-intensive and expensive

» University presses are the cornerstone of the professional credentialing process in the humanities and qualitative social sciences

» Libraries and presses share many of the same values but have different cultures and missions

» University presses need to balance mission with revenue generation to cover costs

At their core, university presses are just like other scholarly publishers with the same important and durable set of skills: the need to weed out good information from bad and shape it to be most useful to readers, and connecting information to the audiences who need and want it. However, university presses also have a distinctive place in scholarly communication—their very existence is an acknowledgment of the fact that a market-based model has its limitations.

First founded by enlightened leaders of the original modern research universities, the history of university presses over the past century or more is largely one of growth but also one of resilience, and the 21st century has brought its own new set of challenges. Along with research libraries and scholarly associations, university presses support areas of scholarship that do not have a commercial return and maintain the high quality standards necessary for professional credentialing. The best of what university presses produce also shapes public conversation regarding enduring problems of poverty, segregation, inequality, family pressures, political participation, education, and a host of other issues with which our society has to grapple.

Since the late 20th century, the decline in overall spending on higher education—library book budgets in particular—coupled with digital revolutions have confronted presses with perhaps the toughest challenges yet. Financial pressures are very real, and while a few presses have fallen by the wayside, many more are finding new and innovative ways to fulfill their missions, often by rebuilding ties with their home institutions and libraries.

A Short History of American University Presses

Although university press publishing began much earlier at some European universities, it was not until the late 19th century that presses began to emerge in the United States. The first American university press to operate under the name of its university was established by Andrew D. White at Cornell University in 1869, with the prize for the oldest, continually operating press in the United States going to Johns Hopkins University Press. In establishing the press in 1878, Daniel Coit Gilman famously noted the common purpose that both press and university served: "It is one of the noblest duties of a university to advance knowledge, and to diffuse it not merely among those who can attend the daily lectures, but far and wide." The press's role in publishing was thus established as inextricably linked to the emerging modern research university: if discovery and knowledge was to progress, it had to be shared.

Over the next few decades other universities opened presses—Chicago, California, Columbia, Toronto, Princeton, Fordham, Yale, and Washington had all been founded by 1910. The Association of American University Presses (AAUP) was formed in 1937, and by 1957 it counted 38 members.

With money flowing into higher education, the postwar era was a golden age for university presses, which continued to multiply and to grow output. But by the 1970s declines in library purchasing of monographs had already begun, and since the late 20th century the challenges to presses have been compounded by increasing consolidation in scholarly publishing and by the advent of the digital age.

Today university presses remain a vibrant part of the scholarly communication ecosystem. As of 2016, AAUP included 139 members across 16 countries with a combined output of almost 15,000 new titles and more than 1,000 journals annually. Presses come in all shapes and sizes and range widely in terms of audience, output, and mission (the best way to appreciate this diversity is to look at a number of presses, beginning your search at www.aaupnet.org). As throughout their history, university presses play a crucial role in supporting scholarship that may not have immediate commercial value, and contribute to the depth and breadth of knowledge and cultural expression in the public sphere. Yet perhaps as never before, fundamental shifts in higher education, the digital revolution, and the decline of bookstores are threatening the future of many presses.[1]

How Is University Press Publishing Different?

University presses perform a unique function for scholars and scholarship. As with any publisher, a university press acquires, develops, edits, designs, produces, markets, and sells content (books, journals, and digital products). However, a fundamental role of university presses is to serve as a channel for scholarship and knowledge that commercial publishers are not interested in, enabling scholars to explore their fields without questions about profit potential. This includes supporting emerging and less funded fields (notably the arts, humanities, and qualitative social sciences) as well as specialized, high-level publications written by and for scholars that constitute a significant portion of university press output. Closely intertwined is the critical place that such publications have as a marker of achievement and prestige for their author, particularly to support professional credentialing across these fields.

Equally important, university presses provide a vital translational function for the scholarship of our institutions, connecting it to wider audiences and raising awareness to inform and shape public conversations about critical contemporary issues. At a time when the public arena is so fraught and polarized, university presses perform an important public service in the pursuit of research and substance. Presses also support diversity of cultural expression through publications of works about the region in which they are based, and from minority cultures and perspectives.

Beyond the scholar and the general reader, university press content has always had a significant readership among students, particularly at senior undergraduate and graduate levels. While most university press books are not written as textbooks, many are widely adopted as such on the basis of their important contribution to a field or debate. A number of presses are now actively acquiring and publishing textbooks, in addition to forming innovative teaching partnerships with their institutions.

Presses also have a direct relationship with the institution whose name they bear—although the nature of this relationship varies widely. In the majority of cases, a press's host institution provides some kind of support that may be direct (i.e., a subsidy) and/or indirect (e.g., office space or technology support). In return, the press supports and extends the reach, prestige, and brand of its institution. Most presses also have some type of editorial advisory board (comprised of the institution's faculty members) whose role it is to advise and ensure the quality of the press's publishing.

While many presses started by publishing the output of their faculty, the majority of press output (often 80 to 90 percent) now comes from beyond their institutions. The shift away from a focus on their own faculties dates back decades to the professionalization of presses in the postwar years and a desire to avoid being perceived as a vanity press for faculty. More recently, the increasing scrutiny of every budget line has meant that presses, like every other campus entity, need to demonstrate that they contribute in a real and concrete way to their institutions. As a result, there is a pronounced trend toward building closer relationships with home institutions, whether through the provision of additional publishing services, supporting a particular disciplinary strength of the institution, or something else.

So What Do University Presses Do?

Like all publishers, university presses have worked to become more efficient, focusing on their core competencies. As always, there is significant variation across presses but many have moved to outsource "service" functions such as book and journal fulfillment, sales support, rights and licensing, and content hosting. Many production functions, such as copyediting, indexing, and composition, are also handled out-of-house with in-house staff focused on project management functions. So what does this leave as the core competencies for university presses? I'd like to focus on a few key ones here.

Acquisitions and Development

The first competency is acquisitions and development. Acquiring new content is a very active role for university press editors, based on cultivating relationships over years and on hundreds of conversations with scholars. More often than not, university press editors have an undergraduate and often a graduate degree in their field of acquisition. This can be important, but their true value and skill lies in an ability to see larger trends within and even across disciplines, and to identify emerging areas of scholarship. As such, editors and presses have an impact not only in shaping particular fields but also in fostering and supporting new ones (women's, gender, and sexuality studies, African American studies, and Native and Indigenous studies are all examples of fields that were nurtured by university presses). This cultivation continues through the peer review and development process as editors select scholars who can best help shape the manuscript, connecting it to other scholarship and to the right audience. This curatorial work is at the heart of university press publishing and is highly valued by authors. It is also in large part what makes it difficult to automate monograph publishing in order to drive down costs.[2]

Filtering and Organizing

In this way presses also play a crucial role in filtering and organizing scholarship that benefits the academy more widely. The increasing corporatization of universities may have given rise to the notion that this role can somehow be taken over by content on the Internet without presses or libraries. Yet it is hard to see how this careful section of authors and content could be replicated with the expertise and experience of an editor steeped in his or her field. Just ask any university press author.

Marketing

The next competency is in marketing, an area that has expanded significantly to include a host of new activities. Publishing the best scholarship is at the heart of every university press, but given the public service orientation of these presses, connecting publications to the widest audiences is also critical. As independent bookstores have dwindled in numbers, chains have closed, and book review sections have largely been eliminated, staff at presses have needed to rethink how audiences find their books. Traditional methods—catalogs, review copies, award submissions, and exhibits—remain important but, like all organizations, presses are exploring new ways to connect digitally and via social media.

It is also important to understand that much of the marketing that presses undertake is aimed at recruiting and retaining authors and not simply at selling products. The designed dust jacket, a seasonal catalog, and an ad in the *New York Times Book Review* all seem puzzling unless they are understood as a key part of brand marketing that helps ensure that Professor Bigshot signs his or her next book with a press. What is at stake here is the reputation of a press and its list in a particular field.

Digital Discoverability

A decidedly less glamorous but essential competency is digital discoverability. In the digital world, managing the information supply chain has become increasingly important, and presses spend significant resources on feeding metadata to a host of secondary partners and vendors. This task is becoming ever more complex; for example, we are just beginning to identify a whole raft of new challenges associated with making open access content discoverable.

The University Press Business Model

While a small handful of presses (such as Yale, Harvard, and Princeton) enjoy sizeable endowments, most presses operate on a cost-recovery model in which expenses are covered by revenues generated. As earned revenue must cover the majority of their operating budgets, presses must manage their publishing activities to balance revenue generation with fulfillment of their mission. (This is a very different model for libraries, which operate on an expenditure-based budget with a pot of money they are allocated by their institution—presses have to fill that pot themselves!) Given the specialized nature of a high percentage of their publishing, presses have always adopted a "portfolio" approach in which other publishing offsets the aggregate losses on monographs.

In addition to self-generated revenues, which typically cover 90 percent or more of expenses, many presses receive financial support from one or both of the following:

» Their host institution—though for most presses, especially those at public universities, this support as been declining as overall spending on higher education decreases; and

» Other external funders. Many presses engage in fund-raising activities to solicit support from both individuals and other organizations, such as National Endowments for the Humanities and the Arts.

The Andrew W. Mellon Foundation in particular is a critical supporter of scholarly communication in the humanities and plays a key role in supporting presses through the digital transition. But although outside funding is important, it typically covers only a small percentage of expenses.

Undoubtedly the most significant financial challenge for university presses has been the decline in unit sales of monographs that began in the late 20th century and has picked up precipitous pace in the 2010s. (Most press directors will tell you that 15 to 20 years ago, they could sell 1,000 to 2,000 copies of every monograph but that today that number is 300 to 400.) There are a number of reasons for this—the overall decline in library budgets, the smaller percentage of budgets available for monographs, given steep increases in journals' prices, the switch from print to digital and new purchasing models such as Patron Driven Acquisition, and the reality that many of these titles generate low usage. These deceases come at a time when presses are also grappling with declining university subventions, increasing demand from faculty authors (especially in support of new scholarship in, for example, digital humanities), and the high cost of staying competitive in the online environment.

The problem of the monograph stems from the fact that it typically fulfills two critical functions: it is a vehicle for sustained thought about a scholarly argument that becomes a building block of scholarly discourse, and it is also the primary vehicle for professional credentialing in these fields. This brings us to the "free rider problem": faculty from across hundreds of institutions each year seek to publish monographs that enable them to obtain tenure but only a tiny percentage of those institutions are paying for this process through support of a university press.

Thus a significant proportion of the losses absorbed by university presses stem from the publication of monographs. While some press directors yearn for a return to the golden age when libraries bought more monographs, a more realistic solution lies with recognition of the limitations of the market model to cover the cost of monograph publishing. The decline in library purchasing of monographs means that the financial burden of publishing and disseminating this scholarship is no longer distributed adequately, and it is time for institutions to accept collective responsibility and develop a new approach (more on this follows).

Libraries Are From Mars, Presses Are From Venus

University presses faces many of the same challenges as the libraries they serve: diminishing institutional support, the dominance of commercial publishers, the growing agenda-setting power of large technology organizations, and the sheer, unrelenting pace of change. Both share a commitment to the transformative scholarship of our institutions, yet all too often we fail to understand each other. At the heart of these misunderstandings are two very different cultures: one facing outward toward a global community of researchers, scholarly associations, and a wider public audience, and the other looking inward toward the needs of their faculty and students.[3]

For their part (and as many librarians have told me), librarians tend to lack a full understanding of the financial pressures on presses and the true costs of publishing. In the digital age, it is tempting to think that anyone with staff, computers, and a server can publish monographs and journals online. And while there is a real role for library-based publishing (primarily as an added service for their campus communities), it is not equivalent to the formal publication process provided by presses.[4] Moreover, the academic credentialing process relies on editorial selection and rigorous peer review, and both authors and promotion and tenure committees continue to express a strong preference for the quality associated with publication by a university press. As a recent study has shown, the full cost of publishing a monograph in the digital world is not significantly different to that of a print book (with the exception of paper, printing, and binding).[2]

For our part, presses all too often fail to understand a fundamental difference in our missions. While the press's mission is to disseminate scholarship far and wide, the library's mission is to serve the needs of its local campus community. As such, a library will not purchase a book on the basis of scholarly quality alone. (When I started my publishing career at Basil Blackwell in Oxford in the late 1980s, the company tagline—attributed to Sir Basil—was "There is always a market for quality." This tagline had been dropped by my second year at the company as being sadly untrue.) The likelihood of most academic libraries purchasing a book that is not relevant to local needs has declined as library budgets have tightened and as digital usage data reveals a pattern of low usage for much of this content. Librarians' response in buying fewer monographs and developing new patron-driven models is entirely understandable but has further exacerbated the financial problems for presses.

So where does this leave us? The good news is there has been an explosion of experimentation with new models for monograph publishing, most of which are founded on close partnerships between presses and libraries (Knowledge Unlatched, Lever Press, and Luminos from University of California Press, to name just a few). At a structural level, as of 2016 the American Association of University Professors (AAUP) is engaged in constructive conversation with the Association of American Universities (AAU) and the Association of Research Libraries (ARL) regarding a new model for funding monographs. The goal is to develop a collaborative subvention model that "will address free riding and make the monograph publication system more equitable and stable in the long term."[5]

A second trend is the increase in both formal and informal press–library partnerships to address scholarly communication needs on campus. In some cases, presses are being subsumed under their institutional libraries (some 30 U.S. presses currently report directly to their library). This can make sense, particularly for smaller presses where they may be able to share resources and to support local, campus-centric publishing needs. Michigan Publishing, under the aegis of the University of Michigan Library, may provide a useful model in which formal publishing under the University of Michigan Press imprint is combined in one unit with campus-oriented publishing services. This integration also creates a hub of scholarly communication expertise on campus for faculty and students. In many other cases, presses are finding mutually beneficial ways to partner with libraries in ways that leverage and respect the unique skills and experience of each. (For example, here at the University of California, the press has a joint Mellon grant with the California Digital Library to develop new open-source content management systems to support open access monographs.)

The Future: University Presses in the Digital Age

The challenge for many presses is not that different from the one faced by many businesses today: how to effectively transition to the new, digital businesses that clearly will be the future and at the same time effectively manage current book and journal portfolios (where most revenues and resources currently sit)? Beyond the financial pressures discussed, I see three core challenges:

1. *E-Books*: Most presses now provide a range of e-book options but this sector is still fraught with difficulty. First, there is the lack of a universal format and the related cost of creating multiple digital file formats. Then there are the challenges presented by new business models and the fact that, for presses, these have largely resulted in higher usage but dwindling revenue. And finally, there are cultural challenges: many faculty and students in university press fields still want print products, so presses (and libraries) are currently burdened with the dual costs of print and digital.

2. *Open Access* (OA): University presses have been slow to engage with OA, not least because the current gold paradigm has been developed primarily for journals and STEM (science, technology, engineering, and mathematics) fields with enough research funding to pay publication costs, and simply does not translate to monographs or the humanities. As previously noted, this has shifted significantly recently and is an area of vibrant experimentation, albeit with crucial questions about funding and sustainability still outstanding.

3. *Supporting Digital Scholarship*: Presses clearly have a role in providing structures for vetting and publishing works that do not conform to traditional publishing genres, such as digital humanities projects. Yet presses struggle with precisely the same challenges as libraries in this area: too many of these projects are "one-offs" and it is not at all clear how one deals with digital preservation. There is a flurry of new activity in this field (supported in large part by a recent round of grants from the Andrew W. Mellon Foundation), and it is another area that provides a perfect opportunity for partnership between presses and libraries.

So what might all of this mean for university presses? First of all, I think we have to accept the following realities:

» All presses will need to demonstrate the value they bring to their institutions in increasingly concrete ways. It is arguable that the strategy of flying under the radar has never been a good one, but it is no longer possible in a world of declining subsidies and increasing accountability.

» Not all presses will survive in their current form. That is an unpopular thing to say among some of my peers, but current trends suggest that some presses—especially smaller ones—will need to reshape their structures and missions to survive. This does not mean elimination but rather a refocusing on the needs of their home institution and building new partnerships—especially with their library.

These predictions may sound gloomy (though I see opportunity in each of them), so let me note two more positive ones:

>> Collaboration across presses will increase. Presses have always worked together effectively for the service aspects of their business that require scale, such as distribution, but this will spread to other functions, especially the production process.

>> Collaboration between presses and other organizations, on campus and beyond, will increase as we are all tasked with serving a new and different set of stakeholder needs. It will not make sense for presses to try to take on preservation—where libraries have expertise—or building and maintaining complex delivery platforms. We will all need to become experts at partnerships, cementing our core competencies and respecting what others bring.

We are in a permanent state of flux, and we can either take the hard route by sitting back and waiting for things to happen or we can take charge and accept responsibility for our capacity to decide our own futures. University presses have always played a critical role in incubating and communicating important scholarship. We now have the opportunity to play a lead role in opening up scholarly communication in the digital realm in ways that will support the goals of our institutions of furthering scholarship and diffusing it far and wide.

Notes

1. Sherman, Scott. "University Presses Under Fire." *The Nation* (May 6, 2014).

2. Maron, Nancy, Christine Mulhern, Daniel Rossman, and Kimberly Schmelzinger. "The Cost of Publishing Monographs: Toward a Transparent Methodology." *Ithaka S+R* (February 2016). www.sr.ithaka.org/publications/the-costs-of-publishing-monographs (Accessed January 2016).

3. Alexander, Patrick H. "The Ant, the University Press and the Librarian. Reflections on the Evolution of Scholarly Communication." *Against the Grain* (December 2014–January 2015).

4. See both Anderson, Kent. "96 Things Publishers Do (2016 Edition)." *The Scholarly Kitchen* (February 1, 2016). http://scholarlykitchen.sspnet.org/2016/02/01/guest-post-kent-anderson -updated-96-things-publishers-do-2016-edition (Accessed February 2016); and O'Sullivan, Francine. "60 Things Academic Book Publishers Do." Edward Elgar Blog (October 23, 2013). https://elgarblog .com/2013/10/23/60-things-academic-book-publishers-do-by-francine-osullivan (Accessed February 2016).

5. AAU/ARL. Prospectus for an Institutionally-Funded First Book Subvention. June, 2014. http:// www.arl.org/storage/documents/publications/aau-arl-prospectus-for-institutionally-funded -first-book-subvention-june2014.pdf (Accessed February 2016).

$$4$$

GOING IT ALONE? PUBLISHING AGREEMENTS IN ASSOCIATIONS AND SOCIETIES

Barbara Walthall

/////////////// TOP TAKEAWAYS IN THIS CHAPTER

» Many changes in publishing in the past 25 years have required more expertise from and have placed more demands on associations and societies

» For many reasons, associations consider publisher partnerships versus continuing to self-publish

» Nonprofit and commercial publishers offer many services and strategies that associations and societies may struggle to provide efficiently

» Deciding to change to a publisher partnership requires thoughtful consideration of goals and objectives

as·so·ci·a·tion \ə-sō′sē-ā′shən, -shē-\ (n.) 1a. The act of associating or the state of being associated. b: the state of being associated 2. An organized body of people who have an interest, activity, or purpose in common: society.

— *Merriam Webster's Collegiate Dictionary*, 11th ed.

Although many types of associations exist, such as those focused on sports, trade and industry, and alumni, my experience is with academic associations. Academic associations, or learned societies, promote an academic discipline or a group of related disciplines. Typically, they hold regular conferences to present and discuss new research (i.e., annual meetings), provide networking and professional development opportunities, recognize career achievements, and publish or sponsor academic journals. This chapter focuses on association journals: their purpose, their importance to an association, and how they are published. For many large commercial and nonprofit university presses, society journals comprise anywhere from 40 to 75 percent of that publisher's journals portfolio. Some librarians may not realize that many of the journals they acquire from a particular publisher are not actually owned by that publisher.

Different journals serve different purposes. A journal may be the voice of a society, provide a crucial source of income (or barely break even, being published as a service to its members), be so influential in its field that libraries are required to subscribe, or be the sole journal published by a society. These types of journals typically publish peer-reviewed or other refereed scholarship in a particular discipline and serve as a forum for introducing, evaluating, and sharing new research and knowledge. Original research, review articles, and book reviews are the major features in scholarly journals. Publishing academic journals often is key to an association's mission to promote the scholarship within its discipline. Journals may be a long-time tradition in some academic associations: for example, *Science* was acquired by the American Association for the Advancement of Science (AAAS) in the late 1890s; the American Medical Association's *Journal of American Medical Association* has been published since 1883; and the American Political Science Association (APSA) first published the *American Political Science Review* (APSR) in 1906. In recent years, many associations have increased their number of journals to meet the needs of scholars as outlets for their research as well as the increased interest in subfields and emerging specialties within various disciplines. Some journals have broad appeal; others are niche publications with a narrow focus and limited readership. Nevertheless, both types aim to publish and share research.

Often, journal subscriptions are a membership benefit of joining an academic association. However, a journal's reach is often far beyond that of the association's membership. Others who are interested in research results want access to the journal's content. Subscriptions are offered to a range of institutions and their libraries, thereby extending readership, increasing citation rates, and sharing knowledge.

All journals are not equal: the prestige of a journal and its impact factors,[1] citations rates, and reputation make some more highly regarded than others. Therefore, when authors submit to and have their articles accepted for publication in prestigious journals, their career path can be affected, including promotion, recognition, and—in a college or university—tenure.

The long-standing tradition of academic-journal publishing continues with new developments to meet these challenges: an increased number of submissions from international authors, growth in global readership, changes in the subscription base, shifts in higher education, and membership trends in academic associations. Open-access journals offer different business models—not based on subscriber fees, changes in publishing models, and new technologies; open access presents new opportunities to associations, societies, authors, and publishers.

Changes in Publishing

Since the mid-1990s, the methods and requirements for producing journal content, and the means of accessing it, have changed how academic associations and societies produce their journals. In addition to technical developments, the composition of journals has shifted from employing local typesetters and designers to those based overseas—combined with more reliance on authors to prepare their articles. Authors' keystrokes now became the basis for preparation of content. In addition, distribution of journal content changed dramatically. By 2003, business models for publishing contracts reflected these changes, particularly with regard to electronic distribution through consortia and institutional site licenses, as well as the potential impact of open-access policies on authors depositing articles in freely available repositories and other web-based environments. The shift to electronic dissemination cannot be overlooked. However, for self-published or partner-published journals, perhaps the "sea change" in journal publishing is the formation of library consortia, created to increase libraries' bargaining power in purchasing library subscriptions. Individual journal titles are deeply discounted to consortia to increase dissemination and traffic to online journal content. These discounts have allowed most academic libraries to provide access to far more journals than they ever could in a print environment.

Two case studies from my own experiences illustrate aspects of self-publishing, publishing partnerships, and many of these changes.

Case Study 1: Self-Publishing

Whereas a number of books are self-published and authors pay directly for production, distribution, and marketing, journal publishing that is managed completely by an association or a society involves a host of additional details and processes. These include manuscript submissions, peer review systems and assignments, editorial selection of articles for an issue, cover design, copyediting, typesetting from manuscripts to proofs, proofreading, corrections, author correspondence, and final printing and distribution—and that is the easy part.

In the 1990s, I was editor of a quarterly review journal, *Science Books & Films* (SB&F), published by the AAAS, best known as the publisher and owner of the journal *Science.* SB&F was established in 1965 as an outgrowth of a "traveling library" program funded by the National Science Foundation to improve science literacy. The journal annually published reviews of 300 or more science and mathematics books and films for K–12 students and a few introductory college texts. It was marketed to librarians, who used the reviewers' recommendations to select new materials for their school or public libraries.

Twice I was editor of this quarterly (and, at one time, bimonthly) journal: in the mid-1980s (word processors were just emerging) and in the late 1990s, when computers had taken hold (WordPerfect!). In the 1980s, the journal staff consisted of me and two assistant editors. Reviewers were usually AAAS members who had expressed interest in materials in specific areas and grade levels. Their information was noted on large index cards and carefully guarded in a large metal box as the way to match reviewers with books or films. Housed in the AAAS Meetings and Publications Office, the journal had the benefit of the in-house graphic artist for layout and cover design and the marketing department for creating promotional materials.

We copyedited the hardcopy manuscripts in-house, sent them to the type-setter (cold type had recently been developed but page-layout programs were not yet available), who then sent back galleys for proofreading, completed by a freelancer. We combined any of our corrections with the proof-reader's corrections. The marked-up galleys were sent back to the typesetter for revision and to provide "slicks," which then were arranged on paste-up boards by the graphic artist. Photographs and illustrations were sized to exactly fit the column widths and then prepared for production by an out-side vendor. Last-minute corrections were cut onto the boards (envision an X-Acto knife and Band-Aids—the original cut-and-paste process) and pasted over the incorrect copy. The final boards were sent to the printer by courier, and we awaited the final review, in "bluelines." Last-minute blueline corrections were expensive and used up time in the production schedule; they were reserved for errors like a typo in a person's name or an incorrect date or measurement. The production process was a tight operation and I learned about the importance of deadlines. If the journal missed its due date at the printer, the window for printing on the large web press was lost and the print job would be rescheduled—perhaps a month or so later. This created havoc with subscribers, advertisers, and renewals; therefore, I did not miss deadlines. I always included wiggle room in the production schedule in case of bad luck or a snowstorm.

In addition to the production process, our small team and the association were responsible for supervising an advertising agency (mostly book publishers and film companies), promotion and editorial strategies to increase subscribers (e.g., classroom science and mathematics teachers), and exhibits at targeted associations (e.g., the American Libraries Association, National Science Teachers Association, and National Council of Teachers of Mathematics). After a few years as editor, I then worked on other science-education and publication projects at AAAS for 10 years. However, I was easily lured back when the editorship reopened. I missed the privilege of reviewing the new science books and films—and then videos—from which I had learned so much. Although the mission and overall scope of the journal had not changed while I had been working on other projects, the reviewer-matching system and the production process were new.

A database, not a metal box, stored the reviewer information, assignments, and comments. The database—rudimentary by today's standards—was searchable! Reviews were often but not always submitted in WordPerfect and copyediting was done on-screen. The final manuscript was brought up in PageMaker; layout, first proofs, revised proofs, and final files were all produced in-house. No more galleys! Ad copy was provided electronically to the printer. New features and a redesign were geared to attract a wider readership. There was even talk of placing older content online! Although the editorial staff still had the benefit of a graphic designer to produce the cover, advertisements, and marketing materials, all other editorial work—including layout in PageMaker—was completed by a smaller staff of two, not three. We were still responsible for all of the content, production, and marketing efforts; supervising the ad agency; and initiating subscription renewals. The editorial team and the association had complete control of and responsibility for the content, production, advertising, marketing, subscriptions, new projects, and new tools. This was society publishing, or self-publishing, 20 years ago. Today, self-publishing offers the same control, with the added responsibilities of learning new technologies (e.g., online manuscript-tracking systems), creating new tools for reader access (e.g., apps and other digital versions), and reaching both members and institutional subscribers. For many associations, the tradition of self-publishing is very strong.

When my time at AAAS was ending in 2000, something major was taking hold: digital access—that is, reading content online. Standard Generalized Markup Language (SGML) and then Extensible Markup Language (XML)—which made content highly searchable—replaced the older static typesetting. XML coding captured keystrokes (now usually the author's, not the typesetter's) for repurposing and redistributing content in new ways: digital and online. The membership subscriber lists were expanding to more institutions (e.g., university libraries) individually but increasingly as bundles, with other related titles, and consortia. Associations and societies had often prepped their journal materials in-house and arranged for printing and distribution. To meet these emerging demands for sharing knowledge, they began to consider hiring more in-house expertise or partnering with publishers to offer more services and reach new markets.

Case Study 2: A Publishing Partnership

APSA has published the *American Political Science Review* (APSR) since 1906. Until the 1960s, its pages included peer-reviewed research articles, news of the profession, book reviews, and more. To give the APSR better focus and more pages for research articles, in 1968 the association separated the "news of the profession" section into a new publication, *P.S.*, which later emerged as the journal of record for the association. Now known as *PS: Political Science & Politics*, the journal continued to expand, adding peer-reviewed research articles and special reports since the 1990s. Both *APSR* and *PS* were self-published and distributed as a member benefit. In 2000, APSA reconsidered the *APSR* and decided to move its book reviews to a new journal. APSA now had three scholarly journals in its portfolio and began discussions with publishers. Why? According to minutes from the APSA Publications Committee in 2001, "Journal publishers can offer APSA more services, particularly in marketing journals to libraries and outside the United States." APSA responded early to the new challenges of online access/XML coding and greater distribution.

In 2011, I became the managing editor of *PS: Political Science & Politics*. The staff was small: the editor, who worked off-site, and me. I was familiar with production processes and all of the steps involved in producing the print product and I knew the importance of effective communication with authors and meeting deadlines. I understood the new processes for proof production and corrections after working six years at a global typesetting firm, which was owned locally but where most of the actual work was done in India. However, what was new was having a publishing partner on a day-to-day basis. The author correspondence, preparation of manuscripts, and copyediting were all in my areas of expertise. However, when the articles for an issue were scheduled for delivery, the publisher's production editor assisted at each step—from final manuscripts to online files and print delivery. In my first editorial board meeting, four staff people from the publisher summarized their outreach activities, marketing issues and advertising reports, downloads and citation rates, and future plans—and then answered questions from the editor, the editorial board, and me. We discussed the unique qualities of the journal, its contribution to the field, and its importance to APSA. Instead of a team of two, I actually had a team of six.

Expanding Services to Meet our Needs

When I joined the APSA staff, the association had recently completed a second five-year contract with one university press and was beginning the journal-tendering process: sending a request for proposal (RFP) to several publishers, both commercial and nonprofit presses. Whereas previous contracts had certainly helped APSA to reach international readers and institutional libraries, the services now offered by many publishers numbered more than 60. In the early years of the contract, many of the production tasks—which had been done by the in-house editorial journal staff—were handled by the publisher. These tasks included some copyediting, all composition (i.e., typesetting), distributing proofs, creating final version-of-record proofs, printing, distributing to members and institutional subscribers, and marketing to institutions and libraries.

As new technologies emerge, additional services provided by the publisher are included in subsequent contracts to stay competitive. These services include a manuscript-tracking system for all three journals; a digital archive of all APSA journals, including newsletters, to offer to more global audiences and institutions; bundling with compatible titles; subscriptions to a broader range of international subscribers; online hosting of current and recent back issues; improved tracking of downloads and citations; and new opportunities for faster publication (i.e., "First View" articles).

In addition, the publisher—with our input and final approval—prepares press releases announcing the journals' new content and, on APSA's behalf, attends various conferences, meetings, and other events to promote our journals. Recently, as part of its promotion of award-winning books, the publisher interviewed book authors and offered to also support interviewing some journal authors by sharing equipment and personnel. My only tasks were to find meeting space for our annual meeting, obtain commitments and authorizations from authors, and to develop interview questions.

According to the *Scholarly Kitchen*—a blog produced by the Society for Scholarly Publishing—as of 2015, more than 80 services are offered to associations and societies by publishers. Table 1 is a partial list of these services.[2] Many are tied to digital services, such as obtaining—on APSA's behalf—digital object identifiers (DOIs) and facilitating Open Researcher and Contributor

Table 1. Things Publishers Can Do for Societies and Associations

Audience/field detection and cultivation	Journal launch and registration (ISSN and PubMed, for example)
Create and establish a viable brand (including filing, protecting, and maintaining trademarks)	Make money and remain a constant in the system of scholarly output
Plan and create strategies for the future	Establish, cultivate, and maintain a good reputation (this is vital to attracting papers and conveying prestige to authors)
Initial funding (3 to 5 years typically before break-even, and even longer before payback)	Establish and monitor infrastructure systems and contracts, managing these ongoing
Solicitation of materials	Rejection of submissions (and in some cases multiple rejections)
Acceptance of submissions	Tracking of submissions throughout
Tracking changes in the authorship environment	Plagiarism detection
Copyright registration and protection	Recruitment and retention of editors and reviewers
Care and feeding of reviewers	Training of peer reviewers
Manage statistical reviewers and reviews	Manage technical reviewers and reviews (see above)
Training of editors	Editorial meetings
Management of peer review process	Conflicts of interest and disclosures
Author attestations	Dealing with authorship problems
Editing of content	Illustration
Art handling	Multimedia handling
Layout and composition	Design print and various online publication versions
XML generation and DTD migration	Format migrations. Just in the past two decades, we've moved from SGML to XML to NLM DTD and now to JATS. Flipping your content from one to the other is not a trivial exercise, and it's not cheap. It takes planning, money, and management to do it right
Tagging	DOI registration
Search engine optimization	Integrate and track metrics and, increasingly, altmetrics
Rapid publication practices	Publication
Printing	Physical distribution
Media relations and publicity	Social media distribution
Depositing content and data	Third-party licensing and negotiation

Table 1. Things Publishers Can Do for Societies and Associations (continued)

On-site hosting and archiving	Platform upgrades and migrations
Native search engine improvements	Journals packaging and sales
Comment moderation	Supplement proposals
Managing or implementing CE/CME/CLE or other educational offerings	Analytics and abuse monitoring
Managing and protecting financial records	Managing and protecting subscriber records
Managing and protecting editorial records	Responding to legal actions
Basic management functions	Construct annual budgets and financial projections
Extended management functions	Board interactions
Create and maintain e-commerce systems	Sell advertising, reprints, and single copies
Manage sales forces	Provide reporting to oversight, governance, tax, and local authorities
Interact with agents for institutional and individual sales	Create or integrate with educational offerings
Conduct financial projections and set prices accordingly	Maintain facilities
Engage in product development	Experiment with new technologies
Conduct market research	Do renewal and retention marketing
Do new customer marketing	Buy and rent lists for various e-mail and snail-mail marketing initiatives
Comply with privacy, e-mail CAN-SPAM, and other regulations affecting publishing	Pay for and comply with terms of publisher insurance policies
Work together to solve more general access and fairness issues	Benchmark and compare notes

Source: *Scholarly Kitchen* (Oct 21, 2014). http://scholarlykitchen.sspnet.org/2014/10/21/updated
-80-things-publishers-do-2014-edition (Accessed October 2016).

IDs (ORCIDs), FundRef, and other unique identifiers. Other services are also essential in journal publishing: manuscript-tracking systems, digital page-flip versions, apps for ease of online reading on various devices, and the ability to reach many more institutional and international subscribers.

The expansion of subscribers from solely APSA's members to institutions and libraries has generated income, of course, for both the publisher and APSA. However, APSA remains the owner of these journals and holds the copyright. APSA is responsible for the selection of editors and approval of editorial boards, thereby retaining primary control of operations and policies.

It is difficult to imagine that a small association staff like APSA's could provide these now-expected features without the benefit of partnership with a publisher. There are glitches; everything does not always work perfectly. Many factors—including our editorial teams and delivery systems—are in play every day; however, we share responsibility for all of these concerns. I need to be certain that the information I send to the publisher is up to date and accurate. Our editors need to meet their deadlines. Viewed as a partnership, I believe that these are mutually shared goals.

Other nonprofit and commercial publishers have agreements with the journals for APSA's 20 organized sections, which focus on scholarship in more specialized subfields (e.g., public policy, religion and politics, and political science education). Many of those agreements contain similar features and offerings for production and distribution. Some organized sections sponsor the journal and provide editorial support and content; others simply offer the subscription to the organized-section membership for a flat fee with no responsibilities for or oversight of content and costs. Some of the journals are owned by the publisher, some by other entities. In summary, wide variations exist in publishing agreements and what they offer associations and societies. However, the goal should be shared knowledge and access to content. How do associations enter into publishing agreements and decide which publisher meets their needs?

Initiating Publisher Proposals

Perhaps an association is considering a shift from self-publishing to a publishing partnership, or wants to renegotiate an existing agreement, or believes that the financial benefits could be improved. Maybe it wants to rebid the journal to multiple publishers to evaluate the competition and to consider which benefits might be gained by a change in the publisher or the current contract.

Most publishing contracts run several years with automatic renewals, providing limited opportunities for renegotiation other than at specific times listed in the contract. For example, a five- or ten-year agreement often must be renegotiated between 12 and 18 months before actual termination of the contract. In associations—where the editorial team often is based at a college or university and therefore changes every three or four years—keeping track of and locating this information can be difficult. It is important to keep contracts in a central location and to review them annually.

However, changing publishers may not be in the best interests of the association or the librarians who will be faced with an array of concerns, including determining annual renewals, loss of access by users, pricing issues that may vary among publishers, and time needed to change library systems and records.

Nevertheless, to illustrate the journal-tendering process, suppose that an association has had a publishing contract with one publisher for almost 20 years and now wants to obtain proposals from multiple publishers to compare benefits and new offerings. What is the process?

First, the association prepares an RFP for multiple publishers as well as the current publisher. Identifying publishers that most likely would be suitable partners is important. Do they distribute the types of materials that the association produces? Are their subscriber lists similar to those of the association's members and institutional subscribers? Would the publisher be aligned with or complement the association's publications? The RFP outlines the nature of the journals, the association's or membership's current needs, desired new features, possible changes in formats (e.g., open access or online access only), contact information, and due dates. Because of the lack of staff expertise, many associations and societies may have difficulty in determining their publishing needs and new trends or offerings and in comparing the various proposals. Especially if an association relies on income from the journal, it may consider hiring a consultant to assist in the project; over time, this cost balanced against revenue is minor. Furthermore, the association's leadership—whether a board or a council—may require such expertise and recommendations yet still retain control or final approval of the overall process.

The RFP should identify several key points and require applicants to reply to each point in a proscribed manner to help the association in reviewing proposals across the board, comparing "apples to apples." A page or word limit is also advisable. About six weeks should be allowed from the RFP announcement to receipt of proposals and queries.

When proposals are received, all contracts must be carefully compared to review financial information, royalties, costs, and all offerings provided by the publisher. Most associations use a scoring and "short-list" process, during which questions arise that can be addressed during the interview phase.

Each short-listed publisher then meets with the association leadership and publications staff to review the offerings, requirements, and expertise. Also, because contracts typically are for five, seven, or ten years, getting to know the publisher's staff and potential long-term partners is important to the success of a future partnership. Will both parties be able to work together and share the same vision? The following criteria are often used in judging proposals:

» Technical strategies and financial arrangements
» Reputation
» Partnership style
» Long-term vision
» Ease of transition (i.e., to a new publisher)
» Cultural "fit" with the association

Evaluating a Proposal

First, in my experience of writing proposals in other areas, I learned that it was key to "know the audience." Who is going to read the proposal? If the proposal is read by a council, board, or others with a modest background in the technical aspects of publishing, a proposal should avoid jargon, be clear, and be customized to those readers as well as the association. Does the proposal reflect an understanding of the association and its needs? Or does it appear to be a standard template with cut-and-paste text from previous proposals or websites (including the association's!). If so, it reflects that the publisher does not value the association as a unique institution or its specialized field.

Second, many associations may give an initial proposal high marks regarding capabilities for the latest electronic publishing strategies (e.g., online and open access), sales and marketing expertise, and beneficial financial terms. Other points to consider include how the journal will fit with the publisher's current list of titles in the same discipline rather than being the only one in its offerings (in our case, political science); production systems (e.g., manuscript- and production-tracking systems); production schedules; and transition strategies.

Third, a publisher's reputation and service must be considered. Having a reputation of positive sales but also an interest and excellence in the scholarship and sharing of knowledge in the association's field—demonstrated by actively participating in conferences, meeting with authors, and sharing with others—should be evident. I was impressed when our publisher contacted me early one morning to inform me of a scholar's death. The news had not yet reached my daily news feed, but the publisher sent the link from the morning paper, knowing it would be important to our association.

Fourth, regarding marketing, does the proposal move beyond how many press releases the publisher will provide to discuss the worldwide picture based on actual data? I have learned that publishers are interested in promoting subscriptions but associations are more interested in engaging with the media or public. Working together can strengthen both ventures.

After these comparisons, the list of publishers may be winnowed down to two or three. What factors prevail in the final review? Maybe two publishers are equally qualified; their ideas—or lack of—for strategically moving the journal forward in the field and the publisher's team might sway the association's decision.

Perhaps more important than the short-term beneficial financial deal is the long-term partnership that provides a strong service component and a strategic plan to strengthen the journal and increase the association's visibility and reputation. Reputation and integrity of the journal are significant for authors, for societies, and for their publishing partners if they choose to shift from self-publishing to partnered publishing.

The Future

Journal publishing, despite its stodgy sounding name, is a dynamic and fast-paced world, with ever-changing technologies and needs. From the competition between large for-profit publishers and smaller not-for-profit publishers, demands from more authors for more outlets for publishing their work, and emerging trends in various open-access publishing options to calls to eliminate print journals, publishing offers much to consider and evaluate. To predict where academic publishing will be in 10 years, then, is rather like trying to drink water from a fire hose. Here are a few "gulps" worth considering.

1. Increased options in electronic publishing will embrace other technologies as well as delivering research content. Comment, discussion, and interactive use between the author and readers will allow readers to become participants in the published research. Publishers will continue to embark on new technologies to deliver more content, in addition to research articles, to include online coursework, webinars, exchange of information expanding or becoming a virtual classroom.

2. Print delivery declines. New generations of scholars read nearly all content on-screen. As online readers increase, the pricing models for print copies will make it expensive to those who desire print. Many libraries and institutions still require print, and because Internet access is unreliable or nonexistent, will have the option for print. Hence, the "print pdf" will remain the most commonly read online product. And articles will be produced to still look like print in a variety of online platforms for several years to come.

3. Open access rises dramatically. The buzz right now is that all journals in the European Union will be all open access by 2020 due in part to the requirements for sharing data for government-funded projects and research. While the United States faces different requirements and, unfortunately, less funding for social sciences, it will soon catch up with the rest of the world. Some publishers are considering only open-access models for newly established journals, unless considerable institutional funding exists.

4. Predatory publishers, those who say they provide quality peer review and publish quality work, will be scrutinized, revealed, and driven out of the marketplace to allow open-access journal publishing to gain the prestige, quality, and recognition as subscriber-based models now hold.

5. Institutions will shift some funding from traditional subscription-based journals in their collection to funding the article processing charges required by authors/researchers to publishing in open-access journals. Or maybe this is wishful thinking . . . In sum, much is changing in journal publishing for societies with or without publishing partners. Staying current on these developments requires continually surveying the literature, trends, and listening to all stakeholders within the academic publishing ecosystem.

Conclusion

Association journals have a well-established history for many reasons. However, as electronic readership, transfer of knowledge, international growth, and new subscription models have changed in the past 20 years, self-publishing associations may struggle to keep up without strong leadership and expertise. Identifying the strengths and benefits of a publishing partner requires knowing what the association needs as well as what a publisher offers and how these two factors may align.

Further Readings

American Association for the Advancement of Science. http://archives.aaas.org /exhibit/origins4.php (Accessed January 2015).

Anderson, Kent. "Scale Rewards, Scale Punishes: Is the Future of Scholarly Publishing Already Determined?" *Scholarly Kitchen* (December 12, 2013). http:// scholarlykitchen.sspnet.org/2013/12/12/scale-rewards-scale-punishes-is-the-future-of-scholarly-publishing-already-determined (Accessed February 2016).

Anderson, Kent. 2014. "82 Things Publishers Do." *Scholarly Kitchen* (October 21, 2014). http://scholarlykitchen.sspnet.org/2014/10/21/updated-80-things -publishers-do-2014-edition (Accessed February 2016).

Anderson, Kent. 2016. "96 Things Publishers Do." (February 1, 2016). http:// scholarlykitchen.sspnet.org/2016/02/01/guest-post-kent-anderson-updated-96 -things-publishers-do-2016-edition (Accessed February 2016).

Association for Learning Technology. 2011. "Journal Tendering for Societies: A Brief Guide." http://repository.alt.ac.uk/887 (Accessed January 2016).

Chicago Manual of Style, 16th ed. "Appendix A: Production and Digital Technology,"
A1–A15. Chicago: University of Chicago Press, 2011.

Clarke, Michael. 2015. "The Changing Nature of Scale in STM and Scholarly
Publishing." *Scholarly Kitchen* (June 25, 2015). http://scholarlykitchen.sspnet
.org/2015/06/25/the-changing-nature-of-scale-in-stm-and-scholarly-publishing
(Accessed February 2016).

JISC. (ND). "Society Journal Publishing Transfer: Guidelines to Help Achieve a
Successful Transition." www.jisc.ac.uk (Accessed January 2016).

Ware, Mark. *Choosing a Publishing Partner: Advice for Societies and Associations.*
Wheat Ridge, CO: Learned Publishing, 2008.

Notes

1. The Journal Impact Factor is a proprietary metric, published annually by the Scientific Business of Thomson Reuters via Journal Citation Reports (JCR). JCR provides a number of metrics and quantitative tools for ranking, evaluating, categorizing, and comparing journals. Available at http://about.jcr.incites.thomsonreuters.com.

2. At press time, the *Scholarly Kitchen* had recently updated its list of things that publishers do to 96 noting that, by 2025, the list may number more than 200. Available at http://scholarlykitchen.sspnet.org/2016/02/01/guest-post-kent-anderson-updated-96-things-publishers-do-2016-edition (accessed February 14, 2016).

— 5 —

OPEN ACCESS: WHAT WE ARE REALLY THINKING

Robert Boissy

///////////// TOP TAKEAWAYS IN THIS CHAPTER

» Main points about open access in the current environment

» Open access is what the government wants it to be

» We have a scholarly information explosion coupled with a scholarly budget implosion

» For whom is the Internet a savior?

» Publishing changed overnight and readers yawned

» Commercial publishers lead in the category of open-access results

When first discussing the layout of this chapter with my editor, the point was raised that there are those who work in the academic sector who want to discuss dismantling commercial publishing and having all scholarly content, old and new, shifted to a completely open mode of distribution. While the open mode is ostensibly the subject, it does seem like dismantling commercial publishing is really the initial goal of some of the outspoken proponents of open access, and to them whatever else follows the downfall of commercial publishing will be acceptable. Most publishers cannot just sit and listen to this. Unlike ice distribution and horse-drawn carriages, scholarly information distribution is not going away, and it is rapidly becoming what more and more people do for a living. Someone might invent a much better way to process, review, and distribute scholarly information, and more power to them. That would be invention, entrepreneurship, and market forces at work. However, you cannot expect a proud publishing house with a long history of serving the scholarly community to commit professional suicide or to sit through rounds of broadsheet and listserv disparaging comments gladly. Most of those who work in commercial publishing houses are simply not permitted by the nature of their jobs to speak out publicly in defense of their work, which means that critics can bask in their inflammatory talk knowing they will get no rejoinder.

While most publishers (and most people) will not sit long to listen to insults, publishers should be listening to constructive comments and engaging in conversation and activities that can help transform scholarly publishing into a more open and more sustainable mechanism. This is only my opinion, but I have maintained it for years. Scholarly publishers can survive nicely by adopting more of a service mentality and by slowly shedding some of their worn commercial workflows and expectations. If open access is going to succeed on terms that both academics and publishers can support, there will need to be a business model. Open-access scholarship is not going to consist of a billion blogs. I would not trust content delivered like that, and neither should any other self-respecting researcher. There is still the need for screening, reviewing, rating, and publishing content of record when it comes to scholarship. A former colleague of mine was fond of saying that publishers kept the notes of science, and they needed to be kept in order. I think most librarians would feel their job was akin to this as well. By keeping the notes, we vouch for them. We do not want an open-access world, awash in bad science. We are already seeing some ragged edges of scholarly publishing that ought to give us pause about what an uncontrolled open-access world would be like. The publishing community needs to focus on what a good and sustainable model to control an ever-increasing amount of science will look like in an open-access world. It is not just distribution that needs to be considered but also quality. Where I come from, quality costs money.

Economic Reflections of Open Access

Ask yourself which products and services that once carried price tags have become free during your lifetime. Ice delivery was once a service, and ice cubes now magically appear from my freezer. But I still pay for the water and certainly for the ice-making refrigerator. Ice convenience has improved, but the initial and ongoing costs are pretty substantial. Transportation methods and variety have greatly improved, but costs relative to decades and centuries past are still impressively high. Grocery item prices fluctuate with demand and location, but are seemingly on a steady rise. Service providers like barbers, restaurateurs, and brick-and-mortar and online shops compete with each other every day, and their prices fluctuate with the competition, but the trend of prices to consumers is generally a gradual rise. This is the less discussed part of the loss in buying power for the lower and lower-middle classes and the more often discussed growing economic divide between upper- and lower-income groups in North America. Underlying economic realities need not be discussed at length but it is important to realize that just about the only things we get without direct cost are those things we are taxed for and receive indirectly from the government. What local, state, and national governments want to do to shape human achievement, health, prosperity, safety, education, and scientific discovery, they can shape. Representatives are elected to legislate what the government will shape within its jurisdiction and even abroad. Libraries offer free loans of all types of entertainment and educational resources because governments wish that to be the case. So when we talk about open access, we must talk about the central role of governments and what they want.

The baby boomer generation in the United States has heard the story many times of the declaration of President John F. Kennedy that we would fly a rocket to the moon and walk on its surface before the end of the 1960s. We marveled at the vision and determination of his statement, and we were excited by the science and the spirit of discovery that followed. That benchmark was an extremely high one, and it seems that perhaps we have been drifting downward since that time in the public spirit that backed such a science and engineering surge. In some instructive cases, as with space exploration and disease control, we are beginning to see the private sector pitch in successfully where government ways and means have declined. If one looks at the money the U.S. government has been willing to spend on basic scientific research since the Apollo program, one will witness a long, slow decline and a litany of compromises with other types of government spending, not the least of which is applied medicine and social security for our rapidly aging population. We can also witness during roughly the same period, from the mid-1970s to the mid-2010s, a long, slow decline in the percentage of total college and university budgets spent on the campus library. We live with the irony of an information explosion and a concurrent budget implosion for the conduct of basic research and research distribution, and we have collectively turned to the Internet as our savior.

I can recall many discussions with fellow librarians in the 1980s and 1990s about the rising costs of journals and the consequent journals crisis for academic librarians. But something about the strength of the U.S. dollar made it possible for most North American libraries to collect in print those items they felt were most needed. While large collections of bound journals were still a source of pride and measured for official purposes, there was a sense that things could not go on the same way for long and the word *unsustainable* was used more often in conference presentations and in library literature. Journal budgets began to push hard against monograph budgets, and the first major journal cancellation projects were announced on campuses. Subscription agents did what they could to improve efficiency and services around journals, but ultimately the journal pricing came from the publishers, and few publishers considered the idea of lowering their subscription rates or publishing fewer journals. As one publishing sales executive explained to me, nothing but a growth agenda was going to be acceptable. I heard this about the same time that I read Bill McKibben's works[1] espousing environmental and ecological moderation—a kind of pulling back from growth as a general social strategy.

Around 1996 and 1997, the first e-journal publishing with scale and seriousness began. Publishers re-created the print journal concept on an Internet platform, and very soon thereafter the flood of ideas around electronic publishing began, and it came from all quarters. I leave aside issues like the cost of publishing in both print and electronic formats, and selling directly as opposed to through agents, and selling in large bundles of journals at a lower per journal charge, and all the differences in convenience between one print issue of a journal on a shelf in the library and one electronic version of the journal available simultaneously to an entire campus 24/7 from anywhere, on campus or off. These realities were so fast in their arrival, and so casually expected the day after arrival, that they define what we now call Internet Time. Credit is hardly given to the publishers who pulled this off. The point is that open access meant nothing at all and was not in the vocabulary before the Internet, and then one day it was in the universal vocabulary and discussion about it became passionate and determined almost overnight. Everyone who has brushed up against issues in scholarly communication knows about open access, about university and government mandates, about the colorful designation of types of open access, the directories of open-access content, and arguments for open access of scholarly research. Endless allusions to good and bad behavior, universal rights, and expected benefits to society and culture from open access to scholarship can be found on blogs, listservs, and websites and amid conference presentations the world over. The Internet was created to facilitate an environment of open information transfer in science, engineering, technology, and scholarship in general, and open-access advocates insist that it must bring in such an era. So what does this mean for scholarly publishers? Can the powerful imprints of the commercial publishers prevent or only delay major changes in the manner that scholarly communication is accomplished? For that matter, can the campus appeal of elite institutions of higher learning prevent or only delay the manner in which new generations of learners and workers shape their careers? Pricing would seem to be the driver of change in both cases.

As a librarian, subscription agent, publisher, and father of three college students, I have begun to see the wisdom of walking in the shoes of others. When I was a librarian I wrote a technical paper for IBM describing how subscription agents made a lot of money and their services must be held up to strict quality standards, and then I went on to describe their services and systems. When I was a subscription agent, I realized most of the money we handled went to publishers, and we managed to make a modest living from doing our work at a very large scale and in a very systematic and automated fashion. Now working for a commercial publisher, I realize we incur a lot of costs and manage to make a living by being very big and working on a very large, worldwide scale and in a very systematic and automated fashion. Smaller-scale models are discussed later in this chapter, but the question is whether they can handle the volume of activity seemingly demanded by the market. Librarians and others have been very tempted to harp on the size and scale of commercial publishing as a kind of evil. Oil companies, pharmaceutical companies, search engines, and really all companies are often perceived negatively because they are large in relation to their markets. There are simple economic explanations for growing a business, and pretty much 100 percent of all businesses would like to grow, but there is a conflict between seeing science as a form of achievement that inherently requires public sharing and the organization and resources necessary to make that sharing possible.

Options for Open Access: A Publisher's Perspective

These comments assume that only governments get to decide public goods, and that those goods are underwritten by taxes. Open access can go in this direction. Many of us in commercial publishing, at university presses, in scholarly societies, and in library publishing operations could imagine scholarly communication being handled by a new business model. Many are trying these new business models. So is open access in scholarly communication anything more than a new business model? Some seek to find money for scholarly communication from other than traditional sources. Some seek to take all profit out of scholarly communication. A few possibly seek to take all money out of scholarly communication. I would argue that you could take most of the money out of some forms of scholarly communication, like e-mail and blogs, and all the profit out of other forms of library publishing, but we still might be best served by having either government, private, or service-recipient money underwriting other forms of scholarly communication. We seem to be trying all of these experiments with open-access now. If we judge strictly by who is placing the most high-quality open access scholarly content in front of the public, commercial publishers are in the lead. What are we thinking?

What we are thinking is that it is better to be in the room while our continued existence is being discussed than to be haughty and disengaged. To be sure, there was a long period when scholarly publishers could fairly safely be haughty and disengaged and it seemed to add to their mystique and even respectability. Universities and their faculty were different then, too, before websites and rankings and student satisfaction surveys. Publishers did not have sales staff. Universities did not spend as much on student recruitment. Libraries did not doubt their importance or having a central location on the campus. All that has changed, and while universal scholarly open access is not any more inevitable than colonies on the moon, it has made remarkable progress in a short time. I am sure there are some who one day in the future will claim for themselves the title of founder (or worse, first mover) in the open-access movement, but the heavy lifting of work toward legitimate open access has so far been done within commercial publishing. It is fair and honest to use the term *commercial open-access publishing*. What we all must care about most is the desired end product—free and open Internet access to quality scholarship. The business of how we separately or collectively pull it off is important but should not take on the constraints of doctrine.

When members of the baby boomer generation think about security in their old age, there are some who might say that security should come from the government as payback for a lifetime of work and paying taxes and veteran service, while others would be fine with security coming from a 401k and retirement savings, and yet others would be fine with some miscellaneous mix of resources. What they want in the end is security, and in fact the variety of means and methods to achieving that goal is completely secondary when honestly considered. The question in the background is whether the government indeed sees the security of senior citizens as a public good. Scholarly communication increasingly comes back to this same question of public good and government policy. The position of government is evolving, and savvy publishers are including themselves in the conversation. But whichever way governments turn, unfunded mandates can feel to scholarly publishers as diminishing budgets feel to academic libraries; it is a feeling of abandonment and a catalyst for change.

Following on the previous arguments, open access is perhaps best explored using the vocabulary of hypothesis, experiment, catalyst, and desired outcome. We know the desired outcome. We have discussed the economic catalysts. We have removed the passionate rhetoric, as we must do with a scientific analysis. What we have are competing hypotheses, which is as it should be. The commercial open-access hypothesis states that if we charge the recipients of a service a fair fee for the service provided, we can sustain a means of information transfer. The ongoing experiments to prove this hypothesis are (1) charge the author(s) of the research for the publishing service, (2) charge the administration of the author's affiliated institution for the publishing service, (3) charge the body that funded the research a fee for distributing the research they funded, and (4) some mix of the previous methods. Libraries have inserted their own variants of these experiments, stepping in to fund all the author fees in some cases, stepping in to fund some of the author fees in others, and stepping in to try to become a publisher in some cases.

Open Access: Examples

In the celebrated SCOAP3 experiment, libraries pay a scholarly society to administer author fees for selected journals using subscription money they formerly paid to publishers. Publishers receive article-processing payments to make content open access in their journals from the scholarly society. The administration of the scholarly society acts as a virtuous middleman to regulate the article-processing charges to publishers. This introduces the pricing regulation that governments would normally impose, but from a nongovernmental organization. Like any experiment, it has not been easy to pull off and the results are still to be seen. From the point of view of ease of process for publishers, it has not been easy. But no one said open access was going to be easy. For an open-access method hypothesis to be true, it may be simple or complicated, but it must result in a sustainable outcome.

The Lever Press initiative is even more recent and has received a good reception in the liberal arts community and the wider world of scholarly communication. While the messaging on this initiative is that scholarly publishing in niche areas will be made freely available at no charge to the authors or to the readers, there is still money in the process. The money comes from the library budgets of the liberal arts colleges themselves, and they fund the efforts of Amherst College Press and Michigan Publishing. In other words, money changes hands, but in a different way. Lever Press can claim innovation and provision of a virtuous service to authors and a world of readers. The works of liberal arts professors that might not have been available to the world as easily as in the past will now be available. The question of whether this will scale up is less relevant because perhaps this is one model where modest spending and modest output is all that is desired. Small sums from existing library budgets are suggested to be the source of the innovation. Libraries are exploring all the economics and redistributing funds to shape the means of scholarly communication. Does it seem odd that a commercial publisher that is seen as part of the problem by those involved in Lever Press–type initiatives should applaud this effort? To me it is a vindication of basic economic theory that when market pressures, like tumbling buying power and rising prices for existing research outlets, reach a certain level, new ventures like Lever Press must be born. And they in turn will have their effect on the ecology of scholarly communications in general. If such efforts can be replicated, the logical allies of the college/university library and the college/university press could turn the tables on commercial publishers.

Open Access: Challenges

What are the threats to efforts like that of Lever Press and the many other library/press publishing initiatives around the world? One is volume, or their ability to keep up with the needs of the increasing number of Ph.D.s globally for communication outlets. Another is the ability to publish with speed. Efforts at the library/press level tend to stress quality as their hallmark, though speed is also a real factor in the scholarly world. It would not surprise me if the most successful library/press initiatives were in humanities and social science monographs, followed by humanities and social science journals. This is an area long suffering from the cost increases of the hard science journals sector and ripe for alternatives. As one collection development head said to me—we need price breaks so we can afford to do some collecting in the humanities and social sciences. Leaving aside the fact that a much higher proportion of grant money is probably directed to this university from the hard sciences, the need to support humanities and social science disciplines with their own resources is real. Finally, there is the matter of institutional acceptance of library/press publishing for promotion and tenure purposes. If these threats are not too overwhelming, then financially I think library/press initiatives have a chance to succeed. Many authors are likely to buy in as long as the tenure committees respect the quality of the end product and the open-access conduit is promoted.

Beyond Journals: Open Educational Resources

What Lever Press does is consider publishing from the author side (no processing charges but also no royalties) and from the advanced reader side (no affiliations needed). But it is undergraduate students who need one thing above all else from the scholarly publishing community—a break on the cost of textbooks. SPARC (Scholarly Publishing and Academic Resources Coalition) research shows students spend on average $1,200 per year for textbooks and course materials. They also offer many facts that relate to these costs being hindrances to successful navigation of higher education. So perhaps an even more righteous goal than liberal arts college monograph publishing—which is after all a very nice offering for faculty—is the movement toward open education resources (OER). Here again, libraries are gaining ground with some funding to teaching faculty to put their own curriculum materials into shape as a coherent electronic offering—thus bringing the cost for e-access to course materials down to zero for students. Programs like Openstax, BCcampus, and the OER Commons are coming into their own, often driven by local librarians and library organizations like SPARC and the largely student-powered organizations like Public Interest Research Groups (PIRGs). It can honestly be said that even within large commercial publishing houses there is dissension between the traditional hardback textbook adoption model backed by campus bookstores and publisher trade relations departments and the library licensed e-book package model marketed to academic libraries, where all books, including textbooks, are available electronically to unlimited concurrent users. A sort of internal market force can operate within publishing houses, just as it does between competing publishing houses and between traditional commercial business models and alternative models. But the eTextbook model licensed through the library ends up being "free" to the students, so should rightfully be compared to the costs libraries incur from paying their own faculty to prepare curriculum materials.

Finally, I turn to the ubiquitous topic in scholarly communication known as discovery. Late arrivers at the global open-access discussion may be forgiven if they gloss over the topic. Hey, if all the science is open access on the web, we can all get to it, right? Wrong. Some of the best librarians in the world have deep divisions in their ranks about leaving the path to open-access content in the hands of a commercial discovery service. The commercial discovery service that needs not to be named is the broad and obvious path for many students and faculty and corporate and government researchers. It has some competition, like PubMed for medical purposes, though this unnamed commercial discovery service tends to drive 65 to 75 percent of all traffic to most publisher websites. Is this O.K.? If so, why is it more O.K. to leave almost all of discovery in the hands of one commercial discovery service than it is to leave scholarly publishing in the hands of many scholarly publishers? The conversation then needs to rapidly turn from just open access to instead open access and discovery. What good is it to solve the one without the other? My strong advice for libraries and their allied vendors is to not give up on their engineering of better library discovery tools and to pool resources as much as necessary in this area. No freshman should be allowed on campus without a shortcut to the library search box on the desktop of their computer. That search box icon should be absolutely mandatory for distance learners as well. I am not an opponent of the unnamed commercial discovery service, especially given past willingness to team with libraries with some applications, but until it is governed by a body at least as trusted as the CLOCKSS (Controlled LOCKSS, for Lots of Copies Keep Stuff Safe) archive for preservation, it cannot be the only way. Libraries vet content for quality. That is not a job they should surrender lightly. Open access goes with trusted discovery.

The Future

» Commercial publishers, ironically, will continue to lead the way in shifting scholarly communication to an open-access business model

» The humanities and social sciences will realize the greatest progress in open access efforts

» Open access and discovery for journal and book content will become part of a greater conversation within a broader open educational resources conversation

Note

1. McKibben, Bill. *The End of Nature*. New York: Anchor, 1989; and McKibben, Bill. *The Age of Missing Information*. New York: Random House, 1992.

6

THE LIBRARY MONOGRAPHIC SERVICE PROVIDER: THE CONTENT TO LIBRARY INFORMATION ECOSYSTEM

Mark F. Kendall

TOP TAKEAWAYS IN THIS CHAPTER

» An understanding of how library monograph service providers can support and streamline library content acquisitions and the collection development process

» The value of the library monograph service provider as an offsite "back office" for the library through their content/reporting database and the provision of cataloging, metadata, and "shelf ready" services

» How library monograph service providers support the work of consortia

» Assessing the true value of library monograph service providers beyond solely lowest book price

There is no shortage of options for librarians to choose from today when it comes to acquiring content for their institutions. Whether it is purchasing from online or brick-and-mortar booksellers, directly from publishers, or from resellers such as out-of-print book suppliers, the choices are many. Each option has its own pros and cons and there may indeed be times when a library patron has a need so urgent that it restricts the options to one: where can the book be most quickly acquired? However, the reality is that most libraries have limited staffing and budgets to allocate not only to content acquisition but also to critical functions such as cataloging and processing. These realities create compelling reasons for libraries to consider utilizing library service providers. While there really is no single one-stop shop for acquiring book content in all formats and languages, through the use of a highly reputable library service provider it is possible to manage content sourcing in an efficient manner that delivers value to the institution and the patrons it serves.

The core mission of a full-service library monographic supplier should be to assist libraries not only with acquiring a book but also with the broader institutional acquisition, collection development, technical, and workflow needs. A supplier's services are designed to support collection development and acquisition at the library, patron, and in some cases, consortia level. Library service providers, much like the libraries they serve, are constantly evolving to meet the needs of their customers. The best service providers are those who approach their library customers as partners, working closely with each, listen to them, and act on the needs of the institutions they serve. This includes serving as the primary monographic intermediary, or bridge, between the library and other participants in the information ecosystem: publishers, aggregators, and bibliographic utilities. Moving beyond a traditional arms-length supplier–customer relationship is a key component of successful library and service provider partnerships and helps ensure there is a mutual understanding between all parties regarding the product and service needs of the library.

Acquisitions and Collection Development Support

Library monographic service providers have been assisting libraries with acquisition and collection development support for decades. The reasons for this are many. A full-service library supplier offers a wide range of value-added support services beyond those of a publisher or book-only distributor. Some of these services include identifying new titles and alerting libraries to them from, literally, thousands of publishers, saving libraries the time of combing through publisher catalogs; consolidated invoicing and statements (i.e., working with one vendor versus many); and customer cataloging records and book processing for physical books, a topic discussed later in this chapter. Further, the ideal library supplier is one that offers the broadest scope of scholarly print and digital content, with flexible digital content access models (i.e., single user, multi-user, etc.), from all leading e-book aggregators and publishers. Larger library service suppliers offer libraries the convenience and efficiency of a single streamlined and integrated workflow for acquiring both print and electronic content.

Let's take a look at how the supplier (1) assists libraries by identifying monographic content of potential interest, (2) matches that content to a specific library's collection development prospectus, and (3) alerts or delivers the content to the library.

Supplier Identification of Monographic Content

The number of published English-language monographs of interest to an academic/research library is generated from thousands of publishers and numbers in the tens of thousands of new front-list titles annually. Publishers publicize new title information through various print and electronic channels, including catalogs, direct mail, advertising, e-mails, websites, and the like. Librarians and faculty are frequently the direct recipients of these marketing efforts, but so, too, are the library service providers. As part of their service function to libraries, many library service providers comb through and analyze publisher catalogs and new title release lists, and, based on their experience, will identify titles that should be added to the suppliers database as well as those that merit further analysis through a "book-in-hand" review process by the supplier. A primary benefit for libraries of the supplier book-in-hand review process is that the supplier relieves library staff of much of the painstaking review of new publisher content. Library service providers, and more specifically *academic* library service providers, should cover as wide a range of scholarly content as possible, including, at a minimum, all university press titles as well as leading commercial academic presses.

Once a new title is reviewed book-in-hand by the supplier (a process that, incidentally, works equally well for both print and e-books), the supplier typically adds additional value to the original basic bibliographic data (e.g., title, ISBN, author/editor, etc.) provided by the content provider. This may include reprint and/or series information (if the book is part of a series); author affiliations; Library of Congress, Dewey, or National Library of Medicine call letters/subject headings; and audience content levels. In addition, content levels are often assigned by the supplier to new books, which can include general academic, advanced academic, professional, popular and juvenile.

Matching New Content to the Library

The book profiling tool is one of the most powerful services a provider can offer to a library. Library service providers can bring invaluable assistance to libraries in acquiring the right content for their institution and patrons. Profiles are refined tools that deliver material of potential interest to the library as well as keep out material not useful to a particular collection. The profile can serve as the engine that drives a book approval, notification alert, or a patron-/demand-driven acquisition plan. Crafting a digital or print book library profile plan begins with a detailed dialogue between the service provider and library stakeholders, typically collection development, acquisitions, and faculty staff. The discussion is designed to allow the necessary collaboration to develop an individualized profile based on publisher coverage appropriate to the needs of the library. As subject interests change or new areas of study emerge, they can be easily incorporated into the profile. A library profile typically has several interlocking parts, which include a publisher list, subject classifications (usually in Dewey, Library of Congress or LC, or National Library of Medicine), interdisciplinary specifications, and nonsubject parameters. Nonsubject parameters can include price limitations, format, and readership content level (juvenile, professional, advanced academic, etc.). These four parts and others are integrated into a unified profile for each library.

When creating a library profile, the publisher list and subject components are typically straightforward. Where a supplier can shine is by demonstrating an ability to incorporate the above with multiple subjects (or interdisciplinary specifications) and specific rules, such as pricing limits, to create a highly customized profile to meet the library needs. For example, in terms of interdisciplinary specifications, for topics where the LC classes might prove limiting)such as environmental studies), a profile can be enhanced by instructions to ensure coverage appropriate to the library's collection. Additional instructions that can help refine and deliver as precise a profile as possible include academic level (undergraduate versus graduate), language, country of publication, and regional or local focus. Adding further value, again, are suppliers that review most new books through book-in-hand, thereby ensuring additional title perspective, resulting in a better book match with the library profile.

The breadth of coverage the library service provider gives the publisher and the flexibility of their subject profiling allows libraries to establish and maintain a collection profile with greater content predictability, precision, and consistency than would be possible if the library worked directly and individually with multiple publishers, book distributors, and content aggregators.

Delivery of Content to the Library

Based on the jointly crafted library profile, libraries can elect to receive either automatic book deliveries and/or electronic title notification alerts for any subject area. Ideally, and best accomplished through a well-crafted library profile, automatic book deliveries help ensure that a library has the right books on hand to meet the timely needs of its patrons. Electronic notification alerts typically offered through the supplier's database announce newly published titles so that the library can decide, based on the alert's bibliographic data, whether to purchase. Electronic alerts can be sorted by several criteria, including subject, alert date, LC classification, and library fund, while also providing libraries with a wide range of information such as the location and year of publication. Suppliers should also provide various electronic downloading options to allow librarians the ability to e-mail notifications to staff within or outside the library to enhance collaboration, as well as to electronically send their selections to acquisitions.

Libraries should expect prompt fulfillment of their orders. Service providers should be able to provide libraries with average fulfillment/delivery times for comparative sourcing purposes. With today's greater emphasis on the importance of meeting the timely information needs of the library patron, the rapid delivery of print content is critically important. The service provider's accessibility to a deep inventory ensures that they can meet the ever-increasing and immediate information demands of researchers.

Access to "inventory" for digital content (or e-books) is equally critical. The library service provider's ability to offer their customers choices in digital content gives the library all the related services expected in the print format. This ability offers significant value to the library. When a supplier presents the library bibliographic data for an e-book, they will ideally include the following information to assist the librarian: name of e-book aggregator/publisher, purchase/access model, availability/status, availability for download to offline device, ability for full-text preview of the e-book, availability for purchase via demand driven acquisitions (DDA/PDA), availability for short-term loan purchase, and availability to consortia and license status.

With the continued growth of digital content availability, libraries have a multitude of content providers, purchasing/acquisition models, and platforms to choose from. Many library service providers can increasingly offer libraries as close to a single, consolidated source as possible for the acquisition of digital content from multiple suppliers. The net result for libraries is greater convenience and workflow efficiency. For example, a supplier that has fully integrated their print and electronic monographic services should be able to offer libraries further cost-containment and purchasing efficiency through duplication control. Some suppliers control duplication of titles published simultaneously by differentiating origination, such as U.S. and UK, or paper, cloth, and electronic titles identified during book-in-hand profiling. Alternate editions of the same title are linked in the supplier's title file, allowing the supplier to control allocation and shipment among various editions of the same title. If the supplier receives an order for a title that has already been placed by the library, the order can be held until it is determined that the duplication was intentional.

The Library Monographic Service Supplier Storefront: The Web-Based Database

The ability to search and order almost anything imaginable online is a part of modern daily life. Since the mid-1990s, this ability has extended to monographic content, and today a librarian can search, locate, and purchase content online from numerous sources, including publishers, online retailers, and their library service supplier. While the storefronts of retailers and publishers offer basic bibliographic and purchasing functionality, the full-service library supplier generally offers, in addition to searching and ordering, enriched bibliographic content, strong reporting capabilities, and tools to help streamline selecting and ordering. Integrating the supplier's database into library workflows typically results in mutually beneficial working relationships with library system vendors, bibliographic utilities, and library consortia.

It is imperative that the library service supplier develops and maintains their library web database in consultation with customers and in response to their changing needs. This includes (1) the provision of a database that provides libraries and their patrons with rich bibliographic content including reviews and title summaries/annotations, and (2) robust analytical tools that allow for the creation and quick generation of extensive and customizable reports through the database interface.

Workflow Support

As noted earlier, a supplier-provided duplication control service can be an invaluable tool to a library. The supplier's database should provide library staff with a duplication check that alerts the user if a title has been previously ordered or shipped from the supplier. Ideally, the supplier's database should also identify and alert the user if a previous order has been placed for a simultaneous edition of the same title.

The supplier's database should enable libraries to create more efficient workflows that can be paperless and save searching of records. For example, library selectors may receive an e-mail from the supplier that electronic new-book alerts are ready for review each week. The selector can review the alerts online, often using data within the supplier's database—reviews, tables of contents, and title summaries—to assist with selection or purchasing decisions. Next, alerts selected online can be further reviewed by library acquisitions staff and, once completed, exported back to the supplier, who will create a file of MARC (Machine-readable cataloging) records that can be batch-imported into the library's system. Once the MARC records are in the library system, they can be run against existing library holdings and orders placed with other suppliers to identify any possible risk for duplication. Records that are not duplicates can be sent back to the supplier as new orders, all in an efficient batch mode rather than title by title. This is but one example of a library supplier workflow arrangement that can be easily established depending upon the needs and goals of the library.

Analytical Tools and Reporting

Another key value aspect that library service providers can deliver to libraries are analytical reports. Library supplier reports should provide data for thorough collection maintenance, e-book usage, and financial accounting purposes. Through the supplier's database, libraries should expect continuous access to customizable, real-time management reports. The reports should allow the user to query the supplier's database as well as customer's transaction files, with the ability to organize the output (PDF, tab delimited, Excel spreadsheets, etc.) to meet the library's administrative needs. The reports should be designed to allow library staff to analyze collection development, expenditure patterns, and support plans and predictions for the future.

The most widely utilized reports include (1) expenditure reports (reflecting the number of books shipped to the library, number of books returned, and net expenditures for a specified date range). Expenditure reports should be sortable by subject (LC, NLM [National Library of Medicine], or Dewey classifications), fund code, and publisher, (2) Library's Transaction History Reports (library's open orders, shipped or invoiced orders, and canceled orders). Transactions should be searchable by date, purchase order number, fund code, invoice number, publisher, title, and ISBN, and (3) retrospective Reports. A retrospective report can be designed in numerous ways, including how possible profile modifications may affect the cost of titles sent via auto shipment. This type of report is also useful in providing evidence that libraries can use to modify profiles to maintain expenditures to stay within their allocated spending budgets.

Ordering

A significant difference and benefit to the library when sourcing orders through their library monograph supplier is the ability to seamlessly link new orders to previous activity library staff has undertaken in the supplier's database. Examples include librarian notes added to the database regarding a specific title, as well as whether the library has previously ordered the book. Another benefit is that orders placed through the supplier system can also incorporate important library local data such as fund code and location information.

Libraries may also submit orders to their monograph suppliers from their local systems. Most suppliers accept EDI (electronic data interchange) orders from a wide variety of standard integrated library systems. Once an order has been placed, libraries may opt to receive supplier electronic status reports to provide updates on outstanding orders. These electronic status reports can typically be delivered in a number of formats, including EDIFACT, delimited, XML, and HTML. Some local library systems are able to load the EDIFACT reports to update orders automatically.

Monographic Library Supplier Database Support

As a general rule, a library supplier's database should be intuitive and easily understood by library personnel with minimal instruction. However, suppliers should provide their customers with a variety of training tools and continuous support for their database. In addition to library on-site training, suppliers should offer online tutorials, telephone, and e-mail learning aids. Specific, context-sensitive "help screens" across the entire database should also be a standard feature designed to ensure a productive user experience. Finally, it is worth noting that the information exchange between most library suppliers and database users is done in real time or within 24 hours.

This is an ideal point to underscore the importance of library supplier customer service support. At the end of the day, the actual product sold by the library service supplier is service and service alone. The best and most experienced service providers have a team of resources in both customer service and sales, many of whom have had career experience working in research libraries. These individuals are committed to keeping pace with the rapid changes in the library world and are ingrained in the fabric of the library and information industry through involvement in library and publisher associations and their related conferences. These individuals also engage in continuous dialogue with librarians and content stakeholders as partners to understand and work through the issues and challenges that are facing libraries today.

Cataloging, Metadata, and Shelf-Ready Services

It was not all that long ago that the library supplier provision of cataloging records and shelf-ready services was generally limited solely to the largest library institutions. This is certainly no longer the case today, as thousands of libraries of all types and sizes are increasingly exploring or experiencing the efficiencies and benefits associated with outsourcing all or a portion of their monographic technical services to library suppliers. This movement has accelerated in recent years due to a variety of factors: reduced library staffing, often due to budget limitations, allocated to technical service tasks as well as the need to reallocate current staff to other important functions. Experience has also shown that even with a higher percentage of monographs purchasing going toward e-books, which, of course, require no physical processing, there is still a need for cataloging. Library monographic service providers have built and continually adapted their abilities to meet the growing demand for this level of service.

Library monograph service suppliers, as part of their mission, work to address the outsourcing requirements of research libraries at an affordable price with accuracy and consistent adherence to library specifications. Among the services that a library service supplier can offer in support of books acquired through the supplier are (1) commercial binding or in-house strengthening of paper-bound books, (2) polyester covering of dust jackets, (3) cataloging support, (4) generation of cataloging products such as spine labels and book labels, and (5) physical processing, such as security protection, ownership stamping, and barcode application.

Libraries considering monographic suppliers of technical services should consider those with experience partnering and creating highly efficient workflows with the leading integrated library system (ILS) vendors and bibliographic utilities such as the Online Computer Library Center (OCLC). With the rapid rate of technological change and advancement, it is equally important to maintain consistent, strategic technical discussions between the library service provider and all technical stakeholders to ensure that compatibility among systems is maintained, and even enhanced. Libraries should also consider those service suppliers that have MLS-degreed catalogers on staff.

The success of a library shelf-ready program is highly dependent upon clear communication and mutual understanding between the library service supplier and the library. At the outset of the process, the service provider will prepare a draft of a formal technical service specification for the library to review, followed by making adjustments as needed. This process will continue until a document is produced that both parties feel correctly represents the scope of the work to be done. The detailed document forms the basis for cataloging programming and procedures that will guide the work of the library service-provider technicians managing the physical book processing. Experience shows that this level of advance definition of necessary requirements and service ensures a smooth process.

Other key considerations to establishing a technical service workflow solution are as follows:

1. Involve the appropriate library staff to review. A typical shelf-ready implementation will draw on expertise from acquisitions, cataloging, the library system manager, and the physical processing unit

2. Question existing library processing practices. Many physical processing steps have pricing implications and may be carryovers from pre-automation practices. For example, if three stamp impressions cost more than two, can the library change to two impressions?

3. Consider standardizing processing practices. Exceptions may be expensive, and they almost always increase the opportunity for error or variance in processing.

4. A clear mutual understanding of local library system requirements will ensure that the appropriate data are in place when the specifications are approved.

Consortia Support

In recent years, cooperation among consortia members has grown to include such initiatives as cooperative collection development and acquisitions. Some library service suppliers have recognized the need to provide consortia and their membership with tools to assess possible content overlaps while reducing monograph expenditures.

Among the tools library service providers offer consortia and individual institutions are peer and consortia reports. Peer reports allow users of the supplier's database to compare their title activity to that of other customers (typically those using the same supplier) by creating their own customized group of peers. Within this group, libraries can generate peer comparison reports, which allow the user to create a list of titles purchased by a peer but not by your library, or titles purchased by neither, or by both. Peer ranking reports allow users to see the title-level view of a peer's activity and how your library ranks against other libraries, by titles acquired, or for given parameters.

Consortia reports allow librarians at separate member institutions of a consortium or library group to instantly see any activity between the library supplier and other members for any title or for a wider universe of titles defined by the user. These reports permit the user to access information about titles acquired or not acquired by the consortium.

Conclusion

At the beginning of this chapter, it was noted that the core mission of a full-service library monographic supplier is to assist libraries with not only acquiring books but also the broader institutional acquisition, collection development, technical, and workflow associated with the book. The level of services provided to libraries, as outlined in this chapter, do not come without a cost and is often the primary reason why book purchasing discounts are not as high as those provided by online or brick-and-mortar retailers that do not offer the customized value-added services described throughout this chapter.

It's important to understand that the library monograph supplier plays a pivotal role in supporting the other members of the collective information "ecosystem": publishers, aggregators, library system vendors, and bibliographic utilities. Through the supplier's work with all these informational segments, the library supplier has a unique view into how all the pieces of information dissemination fit together while assisting all stakeholders with support, guidance, and the unique perspective that can benefit and make our ecosystem stronger. In this respect, the library service provider truly serves as the bridge between content providers and library end users, faculty, and patrons.

The Future of the Library Service Provider

» The outsourcing of traditional library services such as acquisitions and technical services will continue to expand globally to libraries of all types. For the library, efficiencies of cost coupled with the ability for the library to reallocate staffing resources to tasks central to their mission of serving patrons will be key drivers in support of this trend.

» Library monographic service providers will develop new services to support an increasingly digital world. While similarities exist in content delivered via print and electronic formats, there are key differences where the service provider can provide additional value, including assisting with license agreements, rights management, and multi-language content.

» The library service providers who deliver the greatest value to both libraries and consortia will be less focused on offering lowest price and more focused on offering the benefits associated with integrated partnerships with all stakeholders in the information ecosystem: publishers, aggregators, and bibliographic utilities.

— 7 —

GLOBALIZATION AND ACADEMIC PUBLISHING: IT'S A SMALL WORLD, AFTER ALL

James Wiser

////////////// TOP TAKEAWAYS IN THIS CHAPTER

» Globalization and the rapid growth of Internet technologies impact both libraries and publishers in similar ways

» Globalization poses many hidden costs to publishers that may go unnoticed by librarians, so libraries seeking to expand their publishing programs should take note

» Globalization provides publishers the opportunity to disseminate scholarship quicker and more broadly than ever before, which should create positive societal change and broaden human development

Most librarians and academic publishers have very different perspectives on the geography of the customers and clientele they serve. This point hit me the hardest after I left academic publishing and returned to the "library side" to work for a library consortium. The publisher for whom I worked has a large office in London, and over the course of my time working for that publisher, I visited its London office with some regularity. Over the course of those visits, I watched as a Subway restaurant opened across the street from that office; that Subway location was soon followed by a Chipotle, and later by a new McDonald's. I also learned which Starbucks near that office had the quickest lines. Fifteen years earlier I had lived in central London as a college undergraduate through a study abroad program; London in 1997 seemed like a very different place than the United States.

By 2013, this seemed less and less the case. I often remarked that the dining options near the London office of this publisher were nearly identical to the dining options near its other large office in suburban Los Angeles. What shocked me most, however, was very quickly after leaving my position with that publisher, I had a meeting in downtown Los Angeles and was floored by how much downtown Los Angeles had changed over a five-year period. I then realized that I had spent more time in central London over the previous three or four years than I had in downtown Los Angeles, despite living just 34 miles away. I was no anomaly—ask anyone who works for an academic publisher and has to travel often and they probably know the neighborhoods around various library convention locations better than they do most neighborhoods in their home cities. I know the gentrification of Upper King Street in Charleston, South Carolina, better than I know the gentrification of the Highland Park neighborhood of Los Angeles.

Publishing Versus Librarianship: Different Perspectives

As a librarian, I often mentally divided my patrons (both students and faculty) into two broad categories: those who were primarily "on-campus" and those who were "off-campus." The off-campus patrons could be anyone from a commuter student who lived two miles from campus to a student participating in a study abroad program to a faculty member conducting sabbatical research on another continent. Still, the off-campus experience for a student living two miles from campus did not differ too terribly much from a faculty member doing fieldwork 12 time zones away, for pretty much at that point their "library" was a completely online experience for both patrons in the same way. I was a business librarian, so I knew I needed to keep myself apprised with what was going on in the global marketplace to be a better librarian, but the forces of globalization and their implications did not make their obvious imprint on my day-to-day work.

This is not the case today for employees of academic publishing, or, for that matter, any employee of a multinational company that has offices on more than one continent. In the midst of every workday, subtle and not-so-subtle things would consistently remind me that the world is a very big, continuously changing place. Some of these elements are no doubt obvious or could be expected. I am not a morning person, but because I had so many colleagues working on joint projects in our London office, which was in a time zone eight hours ahead of me in California, I would open my laptop on most mornings (hopefully not before I drank my first cup of coffee) to find nearly a day's worth of e-mails awaiting me from my colleagues in the United Kingdom (UK). Videoconferences were the worst, especially when they were planned for 6:00 A.M. Pacific time to allow us to have two hours of productive conversation during overlapping "work hours." Adding our colleagues in Singapore to these conversations only made this coordination more difficult. At any time of the day or night (or week), I could reasonably expect getting a work-related e-mail, and it was up to me and only me to set personal boundaries in determining my work hours in responding to these messages. In a globalized work environment, every publisher is open 24 hours, whereas most libraries close each day at some point, so this was a shift that took a while to get used to.

Moreover, libraries—especially academic libraries—move at the pace of their larger institutions, which typically move to the circadian rhythm of the academic year. Librarians therefore tend to mark time in terms of years or semesters; employees of academic publishers are usually forced to conceive of time in increments of financial quarters or even single months. Practically speaking, this disconnect often leads many publishing industry employees to deride the perceived glacial pace of work in academic libraries, while many librarians think of publishing industry employees as pushy and too eager to move quickly on projects. Both groups are probably justified in holding these perspectives.

Publishing Challenges in a Globalized World

These workplace differences, however, pale in comparison to the more serious issues that face academic publishers because of increased globalization, issues that rarely confront most academic librarians I know. Every academic publisher, and every library that wishes to be an an academic publisher, needs to create a sustainable business model, and something as seemingly innocuous as dealing with multiple financial currencies can create headaches and nightmares for any publisher. For example, most publishers operate using the currency of the country in which they are incorporated. Practically speaking, this means that most publishers account, invoice, and pay taxes in U.S. dollars (USD), British pound sterling (GBP), or euros, all of which are relatively stable currencies. Even when libraries in countries that do not use these currencies are billed in their local currency, those invoices are typically issued at a rate that reflects the exchange rate from a set rate in USD or GBP for the day of that invoice. Prices in library license agreements are almost always written to use one of these currencies as benchmarks.

Oh, Canada: An Example

Currency fluctuations introduce enormous risk and profit variability into the academic publishing business. For example, Canada has a very strong higher education system with traditionally well-funded libraries, and over the course of many decades most publishers have leaned on Canadian institutions to provide a substantial amount of business for their North America sales territories. Over the course of the past few years, however, the Canadian dollar has lost nearly 30 percent of its value against the U.S. dollar. Most mainstream economists lay the blame of this loss at the feet of the depressed global oil market; Canada is a net exporter of oil, and the petroleum market props up a large share of its economy. As the United States has become more energy independent and sanctions against Iran have been relaxed to allow that nation to export oil in the coming years, the world's oil market has become more saturated, which has driven down the price of oil. One of many unexpected consequences for consumers paying less at the pump for gas, therefore, is the dramatic loss in value of the Canadian dollar. As a result, Canadian libraries have lost nearly 30 percent of their purchasing power, and in an environment in which so many library dollars are locked up in multi-year journal contracts, this means many Canadian libraries cannot spend money on new products or resources. Canadian institutions and libraries made no structural changes, yet this reality effectively reduced Canadian library budgets by 30 percent. This is just one example of how currency fluctuations can hurt academic publishers, and Canada's experience comes on the heels of similar, recent situations in both South Africa and Australia.

The Alternatives to Globalization May Be Worse

Unfortunately, shareholders and board members cannot usually just shake off these losses, for the global capitalistic system is unfortunately unrelenting and less than forgiving of such matters. Even nonprofit university presses must face this reality, and perhaps even more so if their profit margins are small. Currency fluctuations have consequences: publishers do not develop new products to serve patrons better; publishers raise prices more in some parts of the world to compensate for losses elsewhere; or publishers make cutbacks in staff, some of which may be in customer service and sales roles that assist librarians with their work. Neither librarians nor publishers are responsible for these developments, but they still negatively affect our collective working relationships.

That said, libraries thinking about expanding their publishing activities need to think about how they wish to set up sales and distribution channels globally, for the way business (even within the library industry) works differs considerably by world region. Negotiations with European and Asian libraries are often more formal than are similar conversations in the United States, and these conversations in the United States are often more formal than are similar conversations in the Middle East or Latin America. In the United States and the UK, librarians have grown accustomed to being visited directly by sales representatives from a publisher, whereas in many other places (e.g., Asia or Latin America) publishers have often outsourced this role to third-party organizations that have better relationships with librarians in those locales.

No matter the marketing and sales mix a publisher elects, the if-you-build-it-they-will-come approach does not seem to work well in this industry. As evidence, I would note that many libraries have attempted to launch their own publishing programs recently, but few seem to be impacting the publishing marketplace with much significance. Publishers invest many resources in building global sales organizations, and while the return on these investments can take time, libraries and/or other organizations seeking to advance their own publishing programs cannot afford to "think small" when it relates to building a global sales approach.

Publishers Are Working Harder Than Ever

Globalization and better access to scholarly information and Internet technologies have required publishers to increase their editorial staffing as well. A few decades ago, the overwhelming majority of journal and manuscript submissions came from a very small number of nations, relatively speaking. Today, most academic publishers report that submissions to their journals and monograph series are at an all-time high, often from rapidly growing nations in the developing world, and each year increases over the year before. In practical terms, editorial staffs at academic publishers have never been busier, and in order to cope with this increased workload, most have been forced to invest in more editorial head-count, more robust author tracking tools, or, in most cases, both. In effect, this expanded workload explains why so many journals are launched each year; librarians legitimately chafe at being asked to pay for more journals each year in their "big deals," but a globalized research community with more scholars doing more research in more places each year cannot squeeze all its findings into the current editorial staffing paradigm and expect that optimal or appropriate editorial standards will still be met.

The additional hiring needed for academic publishers to fill their mission in a globalized world therefore sparks the real, hidden cost of doing business— the costs associated with hiring more people. In the United States, employee healthcare costs have vastly exceeded the annual inflation rate for decades. Librarians often ask why library resources increase at rates that exceed inflation (almost always determined by using the Consumer Price Index, or CPI), which in recent years has remained around 2 percent. Using the CPI as a benchmark, however, may not be the best analytical framework for this comparison. Any company with a considerable number of U.S.-based employees has not only had to pay health insurance premium increases of at least double-digit percentages, they also need to occasionally give their staff a raise or cost-of-living adjustment or risk losing good employees. It is important to note that the same dynamic is true for colleges, universities, and public libraries.

It is perhaps unfair for academic librarians to assert that the increases passed along to them by publishers are confiscatory while ignoring that the tuition prices charged by their own institutions have increased by rates that exceed publisher increases. The costs of doing business in a globalized world whose residents live longer each year affect both libraries and publishers equally, and neither is immune to the financial challenges globalization poses.

That said, globalization has had its greatest impact on academic publishing where it has affected so many other industries: the cost-containment strategies potentially afforded by offshoring. Many academic publishers, more than a decade ago, began shifting many production and information technology–related tasks to India, a nation with a rich tradition of academic publishing and with a large number of highly educated, fluent English speakers. Other large publishers, for example, have moved finance operations to Singapore or transitioned many customer service positions to the Philippines. The debates over the efficacy of this approach can and should be argued (in another venue), but there is little disagreement that this approach has brought down the cost of doing business for many publishers. In fact, in 2012 a well-reputed financial services company's evaluation of the academic publishing industry's largest player noted that its impressive profit margins and revenue growth were more attributable to that company's effective cost reductions as a result of offshoring than they were to increased subscription fees paid by libraries. There are two ways any organization can make more money: sell more products to more customers or reduce the internal costs of those products. More and more publishers each year are adopting the latter approach with modestly successful results. Eventually, however, a basement on these cost containments will be hit, for a globalized world becomes smaller and smaller if you are an organization always looking to move to the next cheapest venue from which to place your workforce.

Globalization, Publishing, and Social Justice

Yet another consideration of approaching business from a global viewpoint relates to the dissemination of scholarship in places where libraries are not well resourced. Many librarian criticisms of large commercial publishers are valid, but one oft-made critique—that researchers in poorer or underdeveloped nation-states cannot access quality scholarly information—is unfounded, largely through initiatives such as Research4Life and its four component programs:

1. Hinari: Hinari is an initiative of the World Health Organization (WHO) to provide free or low-cost subscription access to thousands of medical and health-related journals to poorer nations. More than 400 publishers now participate in Hinari, and almost all large nonprofit, for-profit, commercial, and university press entities are partners.
2. AGORA: AGORA (Access to Global Online Research in Agriculture) is managed by the Food and Agriculture Organization (FAO), in partnership with Cornell University and over 65 publishers.
3. OARE: OARE (Online Access to Research in the Environment) is managed by the United Nations Environment Programme (UNEP), in partnership with Yale University and over 60 publishers, and provides to more than 2,800 institutions access to up to 10,000 journals, up to 20,000 e-books, and up to 55 other information resources in a wide range of disciplines contributing to the understanding of the natural environment, including environmental toxicology and pollution, zoology, botany, ecology, environmental chemistry, geology, hydrology, oceanography, meteorology, climatology, geography, environmental economics, environmental law and policy, conservation policy and planning, environmental biotechnology, environmental engineering, energy, and many other disciplines.
4. ARDI: ARDI (Access to Research for Development and Innovation) is coordinated by the World Intellectual Property Organization, together with its partners in the publishing industry, with the aim to promote the integration of developing and least developed countries into the global knowledge economy, allowing them to more fully realize their creative and innovative potential.

Larger publishers have the scale to enter into agreements with such initiatives, and libraries that wish to enter the publishing arena should not forget about these important endeavors.

Globalism: Concluding Challenges

In 2016, however, the biggest challenge facing publishers may be the search for new markets for existing products. Karl Marx suggested that eventually capitalism would be challenged by the geographic limitations of this planet, for after the markets on this planet are saturated, there is nowhere else to sell. We can easily imagine a future in which every academic library has engaged with every academic publisher (a library either buys what the publisher sells or doesn't; either way, the market at that point is largely saturated). Very few new colleges and universities in the United States and Europe are being established in any given year, and as a result, very few new academic libraries are being established.

In the short term, the best bet for future growth would be in places of greater population growth (India), greater economic growth (the Middle East and sub-Saharan Africa), or both (China). This is not to say that publishers are beginning to ignore their markets in the United States, western Europe, and Japan; those markets will likely be the cash cows for most publishers for the immediate future. To reach profit growth desired by shareholders and/or needed to satisfy rising healthcare costs and other fixed costs, however, most publishers will need to focus on markets far from where they are geographically located.

Any library wishing to expand its own publishing program cannot limit its target market to its own country and any library wishing to expand its publishing program necessarily needs to think about how it will address these issues. Many librarians believe the long-term sustainability of scholarly communication is dependent upon libraries reclaiming the publishing mantle from large commercial publishers. I too fall into this camp, even though in this chapter I have made comments that could be interpreted as critical of librarians and libraries. Instead, I believe the unique mission of libraries may perfectly position us to take up the mantle of leadership on this front. Having the luxury of taking a long-term approach to all our work not only gives us a relatively broad perspective, it also allows us to ask holistic questions that point to the need to make academic research sustainable and impactful for the broadest audience for the longest, best future. Libraries should think of themselves as global players, therefore, for even if we do not want to play this part in the 21st century, we have already been drafted for this role.

The Future

- » The next 20 years will see a massive struggle between globalization and anti-globalization forces; technology will render national borders increasingly meaningless while local politics will likely attempt to reassert their importance
- » There will be few places in the world that could benefit from scholarly information that will not have access to that scholarly information
- » For libraries to reclaim the mantle of leadership in the production and dissemination of scholarly communication, they will need a sophisticated, large-scale coordinative effort to match the scale of today's globalized publishers that is not currently in place

— 8 —

MARKET RESEARCH: UNDER THE HOOD

Elisabeth Leonard

///////////// TOP TAKEAWAYS IN THIS CHAPTER

>> It all starts with a question

>> Every research project should be expressed in a research plan

>> The less noise you add, the more clear the answers are

>> Authenticity and transparency are necessities

I started my career as a reference librarian because the idea of answering questions every day excited me. Nothing has changed about how much I enjoy research but the role I take in answering questions has distinctly changed. I now work for a publisher and serve in a different side of the information ecosystem. This makes every day is exciting, interesting, unpredictable, and challenging. When doing research, I never know what question will come my way—and my colleagues can never be entirely sure what answer I will provide in return because the process of research often uncovers unexpected results and can lead to new questions. Last, very few of the questions I receive can be answered by third-party research. In my role as a market researcher, I mostly conducted original research or analyzed the results of published information to see which trends I could determine. After all, if the answers could be easily found, research would not need to be conducted.

What Is Market Research?

When done right, market research is an unbiased examination of the market, including examining industry and user trends, determining product demand

and what impacts that demand, investigating product usability, learning where your product or service falls within a larger environment, and how it ranks against the competition.

For a publisher, this means learning about why authors choose one publication over another to submit their work; how researchers search and find information; what kinds of information are used; what kinds of devices people use to search, find, and consume information; what criteria librarians use to evaluate a new product or to cancel an existing product; what business model best fits a product; and what price should be set for product.

The answers to these questions can lead to an overwhelming amount of information, if the researcher is not careful. A large part of what a market researcher does is adding value to the research itself as the market researcher helps the organization get the information needed, in a package that is easy to understand, with enough details to allow the readers to make their own conclusions about the results presented to them, but not with so many details that the reader becomes lost.

Market researchers and product developers discuss what audience a product is intended for and how the product will be used. In the development stage, this can seem a bit theoretical, which is why participatory design can be so meaningful. Talking directly to your end users as a product moves from concept to market keeps the product focused on its ultimate potential, even though until a product is truly in the marketplace and is actually used, product behavior and buying behavior are largely educated guesses.

In reality, market research works the same way for libraries and for publishers, and while we may approach the situation differently, we can ask the same questions of the same people. For example, a library decides to be a development partner for a product being created. Because the product is still in the ideation phase, the development partners cannot be sure how useful the final product will be. However, the development partners may have conducted satisfaction surveys and an analysis of gaps in their collection, and so can inform the publisher what they like and dislike about the concept. By serving as a development partner, the development partners are able to provide direct feedback to the publisher, which impacts the utility of the product for the librarian and the librarian's community. Vocal development partners provide deeper and more real-time insights into how a product will be installed, how it will be discovered, how it will be used, and what the desired user experience is for different users. This is information few publishers can understand without direct feedback from librarians.

For the publisher, there may have been more than a year's worth of ideation, research, editorial commissioning, and platform development work that led to the library either beta testing the product with a goal of releasing the product relatively soon or bringing in a development partner to check the use cases. Similarly, the research that libraries and publishers conduct once a product is in the market can be quite similar. Now, research changes from seeking out what might happen to what has happened, but even so, we want to know many of the same things. Did the product receive the anticipated use? Were the expected user groups the ones who used the product? What did user groups like and dislike about it? If the product is not finding its expected market, this led librarians to reassess the product (Did they misjudge the need? Do users know something about the product that the library doesn't know? Are users getting their needs met with another resource? Is there something about the functionality of the product that created a barrier to use? Was the product discoverable?). Like the librarian, the publisher will ask similar questions about the user. However, publishers need answers about a product's value proposition, interface, how well suited the content is, and potentially very specific questions for librarians. These questions can include asking how a discovery is working within the library's systems and if the library is receiving the value it expected.

Product Development, Market Research, and Why the Research Process Matters

In the beginning, a question or a whole host of questions launch the market research process. As is true for any organization, this begins with an assessment of what is already known. For a lead researcher, this begins with ensuring the question itself is truly understood. Sometimes at exploratory stages of product development, the questions may be quite broad and can change radically as information is consumed and the product idea changes. This means that open lines of communication must exist between the person commissioning the research and the researcher. This communication starts by negotiating which questions will be posed, what kinds of answers the requester hopes to receive, and the time frame for receiving the information.

The more honest the discussion is about what the requester truly wants to know and what the researcher can truly deliver, the better the whole process is for everyone involved, including the research subjects. For example, if the research is being conducted as a last effort to catch any changes in the market or if the business is 99 percent certain that very few answers would change the decisions the business makes, the research will not need to be as intensive as when the decisions will be deeply impacted by the answers delivered by market research. Also, if the requester cannot provide a compelling reason that research needs to be conducted, the researcher may ask the requester to come back when they are further along with their research need. Last, the requester needs to be prepared that the answer to their question may not be what they want to hear. If they are not prepared for this or if they are only looking for a specific answer, then research should not proceed.

Before beginning external research, I recommend that some internal and desk research be conducted. Have there been requests for a product similar to what is being considered? How many people have asked about it? Where are these customers located? Do they have anything in common? Are there any trends in areas of research that illustrate a burgeoning or unmet need? Has someone else recently done research on the topic? Sometimes there is enough information available internally or enough third-party research that there is no need to proceed with further research. If the research request remains, establishing what internal information exists can mean that a party can leverage prior knowledge (including knowledge derived from print sales) while new information is gathered. Including and analyzing existing information provides a foundation to frame the answers—and can even help to frame the questions that remain. The more solid that foundation, the easier it is to dig more deeply into a question, and the easier it is to communicate results, as the requester has a more sophisticated base to build upon.

The last part of this negotiation process is to agree to a research plan, which includes determining the research questions, who internally will be involved in the research (and how), which methods will be used, what the deadlines are, and what the end product will be. The research plan is a great touchstone and one that should be updated and shared with everyone involved in the research. There is something about seeing the questions and the methods in writing that helps people think through the research and keeps everyone on the same page much more effectively than a verbal agreement can, especially for research projects that will take several months.

With the research plan clear, research can proceed without any excess noise—the researcher knows the purpose and what needs to be answered. Clarity at this stage means that it is possible to deliver direct answers at the conclusion of the research, without having to continually return to the commissioner to ask for explanations and without the requester returning to the researcher to again express what they need because they read early results or are nervous that their wishes were not understood.

Choosing Your Method

There are many methods that can be used in market research, although the most common are the following:

» Interviews
» Focus groups
» Surveys
» Desk research
» Data analysis
» Usability tests
» Observational studies

Publishers often have multiple editorial and library advisory boards, which are used to bounce ideas off in order to test potential product concepts. With an audience who understands our point of view, a deeper understanding of our work, combined with their own expertise, advisory boards are able to challenge or support an idea in a balanced way. If a publisher cannot convince an advisory group that it has a good idea, then the idea is either bad or it has been communicated poorly. Either way, the publisher knows there is work to do before bringing the idea to a wider group that has less familiarity with the publisher.

Publishers all count on the feedback of customers to know if they are getting what they expect from the products they have invested in. We hope for verbal and written feedback, in addition to the feedback received by the numbers of renewals and cancellations. If you ever wondered why you get surveys or requests for interviews to discuss your satisfaction with products you have renewed AND those that you cancelled, it is in no small part due to the desire of market researchers to determine what is working well and where there is room to improve, even knowing that sometimes libraries cancel products that they like and that budgetary constraints are pitting beloved products against each other.

There are volumes of books devoted to how to choose the right method—I won't belabor the points here, although I have provided a brief snapshot of the advantages and disadvantages to the most common methods. Instead, my advice is to make sure you can expertly deploy whichever methods you choose and that you can express why you chose your methods to yourself, to the people who commissioned the research, and to the people who you are asking your questions (your research subjects). If you cannot express why, then you have work left to do before involving human subjects. Almost worse than choosing the wrong method is choosing the right method but doing it badly. If you conduct a survey but use poorly worded questions, it will not matter if you have a large percentage of your population involved— your research results will be suspect. The reputation of a publisher is also at risk. The research you do reflects upon your organization—doing research on behalf of a publisher means that people, including the research subjects, expect the research to be sound (see Table 1).

Conducting Your Research With Integrity

Personally, I have been surprised to have my research regarded with suspicion at times. I never expected that consumers would wonder if I was really going to use the results of the research, if I was really asking what I wanted to know, if

Table 1: Selecting a Method for Your Market Research

METHOD	ADVANTAGES	LIMITATIONS
Focus Groups	» Exploratory; good way of getting people to talk about their needs, attitudes, and perceptions » Useful for brainstorming » Provides top-of-mind responses and can probe for more in-depth thoughts » Others can observe research as it is being conducted » Visual aids can be used	» Can be an inefficient way of gathering information, especially if the group is not a representative sample of the target population » Requires a skilled moderator or group dynamics (group think or dominant personalities) or moderator bias can taint responses » Recruitment can be difficult without a strong incentive » Competitive and intimate topics are unsuitable for focus group discussion » Can be difficult to analyze results
One-on-One Interviews (i.e., face-to-face interviews, site visits)	» Respondents can look at wire frames, sample content, or other visual materials » Ability of interviewer to conduct complex or lengthy interviews » Ability of interviewer to focus on one person's responses, rather than dealing with a group dynamic » "Intercept interviews" (like asking someone passing the booth a question) can be a quick way to get targeted answers » Use for laddering (successive layers of questions) to reveal underlying decision processes	» Can be very costly due to time-intensive nature » Because of time-intensive nature, fewer people are part of research effort » Requires a skilled interviewer who can guide conversation into sometimes difficult conversational areas and do so without revealing any bias
Telephone Interviews	» Ability of interviewer to conduct complex or lengthy interviews » Ability of interviewer to focus on one person's responses, rather than dealing with a group dynamic » Cost-efficient	» Inability to show visual materials » Probing can be more challenging because interviewers and respondents often feel rushed » Impersonal; probing more difficult because interviewer is unable to watch respondent's face and body language » Harder to use rating scales (e.g., "please rate the following on a scale of one to ten, ten being excellent . . .") » Requires a skilled interviewer who can guide conversation into sometimes difficult conversational areas and do so without revealing any bias

(Table 1 continues)

Table 1: Selecting a Method for Your Market Research (continued)

METHOD	ADVANTAGES	LIMITATIONS
Observation	» Can be performed on site or can be recorded » Shows actual behavior, rather than perceived behavior	» Can be time-consuming » Requires precise qualification for participants » Typically only a few observations are conducted, so difficult to make sweeping generalizations from the results » Difficult to be unobtrusive and known observation can alter typical behavior
Surveys	Easy to tabulate responses Can get a large number of responses quickly With the right sample, responses can be representative of a population	» Can be expensive, depending on incentives » Developing well-written and unambiguous questions can be difficult » Results can be superficial » Need predetermined questions » Survey fatigue » Surveys have become shorter in response to survey fatigue

I was really going to pay participants the agreed-upon incentive, if I was really going to convey what I was told, or if I was going to only communicate the parts I thought were flattering to our point of view. What I hope anyone who participates in my research realizes is that I conduct my research with integrity. I operate my research program with as much transparency as the position allows. I sometimes have information I cannot share with the market because of the stage of research, but if I can share information with our market, I do, including sharing research results. When I promise someone anonymity, they always get it. When I say I am interested in someone's point of view, I truly am. When I promise that I will share that point of view internally, I really do.

What I hope for any publisher reading this is that they will consider why librarians treat publisher research with suspicion. My hunch is that it is largely due to marketing efforts disguised as research, where the only reason the questions are asked is to elicit a quote, mostly used out of context, or when an advisory board is asked to provide feedback so the publisher can state in presentations that the decision was made in consultation with the advisory board. While I am aware that these situations occur, I hope that they are outliers. I am quite proud that our decisions are informed by the information and opinions shared with us, and it is something I hope for every publisher. Letting your customers have a voice in your meetings, even if they are not literally there, creates a different product and relationship with the market than an artificial process will ever allow.

Analysis Paralysis

As we decide the fate of a product concept, we predict the expected user and what they might need from it. From there, we outline how we expect the product to be used. It is from those use cases that we develop the ideal functionality for a product—thinking of what the expected user pathways are and how a minimum viable product would work to meet defined user needs. Should a concept receive the green light, and once we know why and how each target persona will experience the site, product development begins and we focus on delivering the tools needed along the user pathway to help the user find what they need as easily and quickly as possible. We want each experience in our products to delight the user—not to cause them unnecessary frustration.

On the surface, this seems like a clinical, clean process. In actuality, it can be very messy, in part because we are balancing user and buyer needs, which do not align as much as we would like! Before I worked for a large publisher, I thought I understood just how different institutions, their affiliated libraries, and their researchers could be, but after years of speaking with people from around the world, I can say that in some aspects all researchers do indeed seem the same, that there are so many nuances that make putting our market research results together into a useful narrative that expresses what the commonalities are that rise above individual researcher needs, while still looking for those challenges that even if unique to a segment of the population would require a solution in order for a product to be useful. Relaying all of the relevant nuances is not always possible—and of course, the market is in a state of flux, where researcher and buyer needs regularly change. It is this dilemma that can lead to analysis paralysis. How can you communicate a complicated and nuanced answer and how can you be sure that you have the answer when the answers are not black and white and when there are as many variations as there are countries that participated in the research? Does it mean that there are not clear answers or does it mean that the answers have not been analyzed enough for there to be clarity?

DOs and DON'Ts for Your Research
What to do
» Include the business goal in your research plan (e.g., to increase the usability of the product)
» Include your assumptions at the beginning of your research and again when you report on the research (e.g., the assumptions guiding this research are that target buyers are U.S. academic librarians)
» Include the research questions to be answered in your research plan and again in your research report (the general questions that are expected to be answered in each phase of the research)
» Include the expected time frame and market research responsibilities in your research plan and in any research updates you provide. For each category of the research questions, determine when and how the questions will be answered, as well as who will be answering the questions— then communicate the status of your research with the time frame and responsibilities
» Take notes that capture what the research subjects are saying, not what you are thinking. Having the ability to separate your thoughts from theirs is invaluable and it is very difficult to reconstruct later.
» Be present. If you are conducting a focus group or interview, while you need to be thinking about your next question, your subject will disengage if you are obviously disengaged or it feels like you are just going through the motions.
» Knowing what a good answer should sound like will help you write questions and know when an answer can be considered complete

What not to do
» Don't believe that the person commissioning the research knows what they need (e.g., the initial question posed may not resemble the final question that you are answering)

>> Don't assume that you are unbiased. Instead, acknowledge where you may believe you already know an answer or that you want a particular answer to be uncovered.

>> Don't assume that your language will be understood by every user group. Not only are there regional variations in phrasing, there are professional differences as well. Figure out what they are by pre-testing your questions with members of the community you are trying to reach.

>> Don't believe that you cannot adjust your research. If something is not working, don't stick with it! You can abort a project, change methods, or determine if someone else should be involved in the project.

>> Don't analyze the responses in the midst of an interview or focus group. Your analysis should be conducted after your research is completed. If you analyze too early, you start seeing your answer in every new bot of information you receive, rather than analyzing the whole picture.

What's Next: Working Together

For libraries and for publishers, new products can be a costly venture. Because of the investment involved, both parties are likely to conduct research before and after making the investment, and even though they are studying the same product, research questions will be just different enough to lead to differing research approaches, data, and conclusions. Although libraries and publishers tend to avoid collaborations when conducting research, there is such potential in using big data to learn more about how users conduct research, what their stumbling blocks are, and what kinds of information they need more and less of.

Ideally, publishers and libraries will work together to answer questions about how information resources are used, sharing what we can so that the products we produce and that libraries acquire can be both useful and used, all for the good of the users we share an interest in serving, and in ways that do not violate individual privacy.

This collaboration can include sharing the results of research where possible, libraries serving as development partners with publishers, publishers creating use cases for a product in concert with user and buyer feedback—and in the end, all of the stakeholders sharing what matters to each in the information ecosystem. In order for this to work optimally, each party must let down their guard so that they can learn from and appreciate the other's experiences.

Last, librarians are themselves consumers. This unique relationship should provide less of a barrier and more of a codevelopment atmosphere. Imagine if that cooperation began with the research—product research initiated more like it was open innovation, calling for users to help seek solutions to the problems that plague them with compensation for each resolved research question!

The Future

Market research can seem easy to conduct. That has led to an environment where survey fatigue is prevalent (partially due to a reliance on poorly written surveys) and to the function of market research either being eliminated or incorporated into many other job roles, such as marketing managers, product managers, or editors. At the same time, consumers of all types are confronted with a deluge of requests for information about what they want and do. In this environment, I predict that there are three potential ramifications for publishers:

>> Participants in publisher's traditional market research efforts (focus groups, surveys, and interviews) will demand more than financial remuneration in order to participate in the research. This could include asking for brief summaries of lessons learned from the research or illustrations of how the research changed an existing product.

>> Because of a decline in market research positions in publishing companies, the most common form of market research will be usability tests that help the publisher make decisions about changes to product platforms

>> Publishers who rigorously analyze the industry, their customers' needs, and their own sales and usage data will have a competitive advantage, especially those comfortable with big data

» Publishers will learn to use market research to tell the story of their users internally to stakeholders who rarely meet the end users. By leveraging the art of storytelling, decision making will be informed with the end user in mind.

9

MAKING BEAUTIFUL MUSIC: THE ROLE OF A PUBLISHER IN THE WORLD OF JOURNALS

Jayne Marks

 TOP TAKEAWAYS IN THIS CHAPTER

» Publishing a successful journal is all about balancing competing needs

» Growth in the number of researchers and their output continues to place strain on the journal ecosystem

» Good quality information costs money to produce

» The big deal, pay per view, and article processing charges are all ways to deliver content to those who need to read it

» Publishers provide a service to validate and deliver journals in a way that can be discovered and trusted

So what do publishers really do? This is a question that I have been asked throughout my years as a journal publisher. And sometimes it seems that as journal publishing becomes more challenging and ever more complex, the prevailing idea is that publishers do very little. When I am talking to a potential recruit, I describe the role as being akin to the conductor of an orchestra. You have to bring together many different players and create a harmonious output, and the different players have many different, sometimes competing needs that have to be balanced.

The Authors

The motivation of an author varies throughout their career. In the early days, publishing journal articles is a vital component to achieving tenure.

Even today, many of the tenure boards are looking for evidence of publishing in journals with a certain "impact factor.[1]" In China, a publication in a journal with an Impact Factor is a recent requirement in achieving a Ph.D., which has driven the submissions from that region even higher. Once tenure is achieved, journal publications are important outputs from grant-funded research, particularly in the basic sciences, and help authors to secure the next research grant. Authors are generally keen to be published in the most prestigious journal relevant to the content of their work. If the results are truly groundbreaking, the author has a better chance of being published in a highly ranked, broad-based journal. But if the work builds on the existing body of literature it is more likely to be accepted by a specialist publication. One interesting dilemma that authors and publishers face is where and how to publish negative results; that is, research that proves something does not work. These papers[2] are an important addition to the literature but not popular with editors of journals. This makes these papers good candidates for open access journals.

Having ones work read is important, but it is particularly critical for authors to be read by their peers. This tends to create loyalty to a specific publication or professional society's publications. Another factor that can impact the choice of where to publish can be the speed of peer review and thus publication. This is more likely to be important in the basic sciences and relatively less so, for example, in the humanities. And open access? Well, this seems to be driven by funder mandate, custom and practice in a discipline (for example, computational biology), and less by personal ideology. The funding bodies that award grants for research increasingly dictate that the output of that research be freely available for anyone to read. Having the option to go open access in the so-called hybrid model is now essential in medical and life science publishing, where the bulk of research funding is spent.

So what do authors need from publishers? They need a system for uploading and tracking their paper. Authors have varying needs for copyediting support and for a fast and efficient publication process. Once published, authors want to be sure that the paper can be found—generally through a Google Scholar search, and often through a subject-specific search tool such as PubMed Central.[3] This might include uploading the paper to a repository of some kind on behalf of the author. Having the brand recognition of a journal attached to their published work can be critical to some authors. And of course, authors want to know that peers will be able to read the article either as a member of a professional society or within an institution's network. In some disciplines, having a print output is also still important, for example, in many medical disciplines where market research shows that readers prefer to browse journals in print.

The Editor/Editor-in-Chief

The most important thing to know about editors is that they generally have total discretion over what is selected for publication. In most cases the number of papers submitted to the journal far exceeds the number that can be published in the space allowed. It is generally clear when a paper is completely unacceptable—either it is out of scope or not of sufficient quality for the publication. The editor may in this case reject a paper out of hand. The majority of papers are sent to peer reviewers, generally two or three, to solicit views on the quality of the work. Finding and keeping good peer reviewers is one of the most important roles of the editor. It is the editor's job to adjudicate between peer reviewer comments and to ensure that the author revises their paper to respond to reviewer recommendations. It is also increasingly important to gauge whether an article is plagiarizing another's work or contains fraud in some way.

Publishers provide editors with systems and services to support their work and information to help improve their journal. These services include the peer-review system, which allows efficient processing of papers, and generally a system for tracking papers through the production system to publication. Journals and publishers vary enormously in how much or how little work is done on a paper before publication. Copyediting, language improvement, image redrawing/re-lettering, and proofreading used to be standard but are now more variable. They may be replaced or supplemented by services that upload and store additional data, such as data sets and videos that the authors choose to include with their work. Standard services now can include automated checking of references and linking them to the relevant source, and optional services include systems that allow checking content for plagiarism.

Online hosting systems for journals often provide editors with the ability to gather selections of related papers into special collections. Editorial commentary, letters from readers, and links to additional information are all services that can be enabled by publishers' systems. New tools and online enhancements are frequently launched. Editors want to make sure that their journal keeps up with its competitors, putting pressure on the publisher to provide these new features. Recently journals have been adding the ability to "like" papers, add open comments post-publication, or post links to social media.

And last, but perhaps most important, the publisher will provide the editor with an agreed number of pages to publish the accepted content. As the volume of submissions grows, editors are under pressure to publish more and more to avoid ever-increasing rejection rates: often journals can only publish a small percentage of the articles submitted. This pressure can be relieved by adding pages or issues to the journal, but it can also lead to requests from editors to launch new companion journals to meet the needs of critical author groups.

The Society Owner

Many journals are owned by professional or academic societies or associations. For many such nonprofit organizations, their journal(s) provide much-needed income, particularly as their second source of income—annual meetings—are often in decline. Societies contract with publishers, either university presses or commercial publishers, to provide a wide range of services, with the contracts generally ranging from five to ten years. Typically, the society appoints the editor but most of the publication process is managed by the publisher. Society contracts are highly competitive with specialist consultants often managing the process for the society. Publishers are expected to provide financial support in a number of different ways, depending on the size of the journal. This can include the cost of supporting the editor and editorial office, editorial board meetings and strategy meetings, a percentage of revenue or profit as a royalty, and often an up-front signing bonus. This financial support to the society is often an important consideration when renewing a publisher contract and can be part of the reason why a society decides to change publishers for its journals.

The role of the publisher in managing society journals can vary enormously from being a simple service provider to a strategic partner who can provide information and advice on how best to improve the journal. This can include a detailed analysis of citation data to identify areas for improvement or expansion and in-depth market research to better understand what members want from their society publication. As societies look for avenues to grow and better serve their members, they often turn to their journal and publishing partners with ideas for launching new sections of a journal or completely new journals. Publishers will then help with undertaking market research and analyzing the published literature to help identify opportunities for new publications. Finding ways to fund these requests for expansion is a key task of any publisher and likely explains some of the recent growth in dedicated new open access journals.

The Reader

There was a time when individuals would subscribe to one or two journals, perhaps get copies of their society journal, and then read these cover-to-cover in print. Apart from a small number of disciplines where readers still want to receive print, most readers now access journal content online, generally through their institution. This allows readers to scan more titles and select specific articles of interest. Research in the medical space, for example, has shown that today's users are reading more articles than they did a few years ago.[4] Sophisticated search engines allow the reader to select exactly what they want to read and have an alert sent to them once something of interest has published. While this allows the reader to be more efficient and fully research a subject, editors are concerned that the serendipity of finding something of interest while browsing a table of contents, for example, is rapidly becoming a thing of the past.

As the overall volume of published material continues to grow relentlessly, the reader/researcher is challenged to stay on top of topics and articles they should read. And knowing what content is trustworthy or worth their time is more difficult as the number of journals grows. This often means that the brand name of a journal is critical.

The Subscriber/Librarian

The librarian is generally the journal publisher's most important customer. Librarians rightly have strong views about the quality and scope of publications and about the inevitable cost of acquiring what they need for their patrons. As the volume of research continues to expand, the number of research articles grows, along with the size of existing journals and the number of new journals. The available purchasing funds never keep pace with this expansion, leading to a budget crunch. For example, in challenging economic times, library budgets often do not keep up with inflation, the Producer Price Index (PPI), or the changing currency value. This means librarians face hard decisions to exist without needed resources and generally do not like to cancel journals, as they know they can rarely get back funding for them. Publishers have responded in different ways to try to help.

The first step was to go online. The vast majority of journals are now available online and this saves on shelf space and allows for greater access outside the library. I am often asked why publishers do not simply stop printing altogether. In some disciplines, this has already happened, for example, in basic sciences but in others, for example, humanities and clinical medicine, readers often still demand print. In the case of clinical medicine, if a journal is to secure advertising it will need to maintain a certain number of editorial pages. Marketing professionals rely on services such as Kantar,[4] which only measures print readership. Without revenue from advertising to help subsidize costs, the price of a subscription to the journal would inevitably rise.

Larger publishers then offered bundles of journals—the so-called big deal—which provided more content for a deep discount over the combined list price. There have been concerns about big deals, mainly about the percentage of available library funds that they take up. But there is no doubt that overall, more content is made available to an individual library patron. Of course, librarians will then weigh the amount of content against the usage that it gets from patrons. So how do publishers arrive at a price for these bundled deals? There are probably as many methods as there are publishers, but generally there is a formula for each institution based on a mix of some or all of the following: institution size, geographical location, type of institution (research or teaching; classification, e.g., Carnegie classification; academic or corporate; hospital or medical school), historical spending on individual subscriptions, usage, content mix, and growth.

Sometimes these elements are weighted by importance. Publishers will often undertake periodic analyses to ensure that institutions of similar characteristics are paying roughly similar amounts for the same content and adjust prices accordingly. But in the end, there is often a negotiation between the librarian and the sales rep from the publisher or distributor leading to an agreed price and an accompanying license governing what can be done with the content. Recently publishers have been reducing the subscription price for some journals because of the amount of open access content it contains, sometimes termed open access offsetting. Because of the number of possible variables and the fact that publishers do not follow a standard model, the setting of prices for big deals can seem opaque.

As librarians have come under more pressure from budget cuts, publishers commonly offer a token-based model of some kind that allows the librarian to offer access to everything but only pay for what they use.

Back in the 1980s, publishers typically issued a list of journal titles and prices to subscription agents once a year and wait to see how many orders come in over the winter months. Issues were then shipped either direct to the institution or to the subscription agent. There was no need for a dedicated sales force or anyone to manage licenses. Prices were simple and transparent and revenue highly predictable. Today, publishers need either an international network of distributors and agents or a full international sales force of people in all regions, or perhaps a mix of these two approaches depending on geographic region. Prices have to be calculated and set almost at the individual customer level and might cover print or online or both. Then a customer service team will ensure that the institution is able to set up its journals within its discovery service and make them available to end users. Monthly usage reporting is provided to all customers in line with the requirements of counter. To add even more complexity on both sides, the librarian might also manage article processing charges for the open access publications from its patrons.

The Research Funder

The role of the funder of research as a stakeholder in the journal publishing process is a relatively recent phenomenon. Many research bodies now have policies covering how the output of their funded research should be published, disseminated, and tracked. Publishers now track these requirements and provide a range of payment and licensing options to authors to ensure they are able to comply.

Public and private funders are under increased scrutiny and pressure to measure the outcomes of their funded research for accountability to government, the public, and to assure and measure dissemination within the scientific community. Doing this through the published results of funded studies is thus fostering new metrics and evaluation tools.

The Publisher

The essential role of a publisher is to help make a journal the best it can be. But what does it mean to be the best? Being the biggest? Having the highest impact factor? Being the fastest to publish new work? Being the one with the most online tools and features? Being the cheapest? Delivering the highest financial return to its owner? Publishing exactly what the reader wants to read? The answer of course depends very much on which stakeholder you are talking to.

As far as an author is concerned, the best journal might offer the best peer reviewers, have the fastest publication time, have the most prestigious brand, be read by a critical group of peers, or have the lowest article processing charges. But a single journal is unlikely to be able to meet all of these criteria. A publisher, working with the editor and, if appropriate, the society owner, will set goals for the journal. Much like the conductor of an orchestra will set out to produce the best piano concerto or opera, a publisher will aim for their journal to be the most highly cited or perhaps meet the needs of the society members. So how do they do this and balance the competing needs?

The first step in strategic planning is to understand where you are now. To do so, the publisher will undertake a detailed analysis of all available metrics. These will include citation data, usage data at both the article and journal level, geographic analysis of both authors and readers, subscription information and trending, and of course, financial data indicating the future viability of the journal. This analysis will likely raise some key questions that could be answered by conducting market research. Reader and author surveys are commonly undertaken. An editor might poll editorial board members for feedback on content, and societies will generally want to know what its members think of the journal.

It is the publisher's job to pull together all of this data, which will then be used to review and revise the strategic plan for the journal. Generally this is done with the editor and key editorial team members but will also involve the wider team within the publishing company including representatives from marketing, production, sales, and finance. In the case of a society journal, this process will generally be driven by the society.

A good strategic plan will cover all aspects of the journal and will strive to balance and resolve some of the competing pressures. Key elements will include the following.

Selection of Content

An important question is "is the journal publishing the right content?" Reader and author surveys will help give the editor feedback about what they are accepting for publication. But this is also often guided by the journal's impact factor ambitions. If the journal is striving to be a highly cited, prestigious title, publishing only the "best" research, that will mean accepting only papers that are novel and groundbreaking so they will be cited by new authors. However, a higher impact factor is going to attract a higher number of papers to be submitted. This can lead to an ever-increasing rejection rate, sometimes as high as 90 percent. Once a journal's rejection rate becomes very high, there is usually a need to relieve the pressure with additional pages and/or the launch of a spin-off journal. The cost of rejecting so many papers is high, both in financial terms and in time required from the editor and peer reviewers. Alternatively, adding additional pages or launching a new journal also require additional investment.

Not every journal can be as selective and as a result, some journals set out to meet other needs in the market. This could be done perhaps to offer a very fast publication time for highly time-sensitive research, or they might focus on a narrow subject area of specialist interest. Society journals often set a goal of offering their members somewhere to publish while also offering content to read that is of interest. Finding and attracting the papers that a journal really wants to publish is generally driven by a marketing function through e-mail campaigns.

One new area of concern to many editors and publishers is the increasing incidence of fraud in submitted content. Journals are receiving more articles that contain plagiarized content, images and data sets that have been fabricated, coauthors who have not been involved in conducting the research, ghost authors not named on the paper, and even fake recommended reviewers. There are tools that can help detect plagiarism but other problems can only be uncovered by vigilant editors, managing editors, peer reviewers, and production editors.

Dissemination of Journal Content

A vital element of the strategic plan is how to ensure that the maximum number of readers can find and read the journal content. Where once this was a relatively simple choice of where to print the journal, on what paper, and how best to distribute the physical copies, publishers now have to decide where to host the online content and how to ensure it is discoverable. Publishers generally adopt a build or license approach, depending on size. Smaller publishers and larger self-published societies often use platforms such as High-Wire or Atypon, whereas larger publishers tend to build and maintain their own platforms. Wherever the journal is hosted, the brand of the title needs to be attached to the article. This helps in two ways: the reader knows to what extent they can trust the article, and the journal is benefited by getting its name out to possible new authors.

An online version of the journal can be much more than a collection of individual papers. One of the first major enhancements publishers made was to link references at the end of papers to its original hosted location, using a system called CrossRef. Publishers have also digitized archived versions of journals to add to a subscription an institution is purchasing. Additional content can also be added to an online version of an article, called supplemental content. This supplemental content might be Powerpoint slides, data sets, additional images, or even video, and is generally aimed at enriching the content for the individual reader. For authors wishing to make full research data available to readers, commercial services are now offered by publishers to host this content, such as Dryad and Figshare.

Now that there is so much content available online, editors and publishers have started to add contextual material to enhance information in articles. This could include podcasts from the editor or author, explaining the context to the article. It could be a video, video collections, or even curated collections of articles from multiple issues on a specific topic. In some disciplines this might include continuing education options like journal clubs and continuing medical education credits for completing assessments online.

But how does a reader find all of this content? One of the key parts of an article's production today is the creation of metadata that accompanies the article. This will typically be the title, journal title, bibliographic reference, authors' names and affiliations, the abstract and keywords, and/or semantic tags. This metadata is distributed by the publisher to multiple destinations to improve discovery of the article. Metadata standards themselves are constantly evolving so publishers need to constantly monitor and remain up to date. For example, many libraries now use proprietary discovery services to help find content across the many platforms they subscribe to, and publishers need to send their metadata to these services or their content will essentially become invisible within the library network. In addition, publishers will generally enable Google and Google Scholar, indexing of the full text of the journals to help general discovery of this metadata. Each article is also assigned a unique identifier—a digital object identifier (DOI)—which allows it to be linked to from future papers that might cite it in a reference link.

Once an article or issue is published online, the publisher will use a number of ways to ensure that key readers will be able to find and read the article. The public can register to receive an e-mail with the table of contents for an issue, or a publisher might send an e-mail blast to registered readers who might be interested in a specific article. On the online version of any article, there will generally be a link to "more papers like this," "papers that have cited this paper," and so on to help readers find related content. Authors are encouraged to promote their work with a link to the online version, and new tools are available to help with this and to track success, such as Kudos and alternative metrics (e.g., Altmetrics).

Probably the most important new area of development for journal publishing in the 2010s has been mobility—being able to offer access on smartphones and tablets. Many journals offer dedicated apps of their journals, which are available to individuals, and some offer institutional access through services such as Browzine. More recently, users have moved away from stand-alone apps and tend to prefer the online browsing experience offered by newer responsive design technologies. Journals now need to be available as the original print, online, and app versions and in a responsive mode for smartphones and tablets of all sizes.

In addition to these services, which are now generally the basics offered by most publications, new features and functions are often offered by start-up companies. There have been a number of experiments using enhanced PDF files, which are designed to give the ease of use of a PDF with additional search or enhanced content ability. Images can be embedded as 3-D, interactive, or even virtual reality. Video can be offered embedded in the file. New features like these rarely become standard across journal publishers but they can provide important enhancements for certain disciplines.

Financial Viability

Once a publisher has a plan for which content to publish and how much, it is critical to balance the journal costs with the income. Over the years, this equation has become ever more complex, with costs and revenue shifting from traditional areas to new, more variable options. Let us look at production, for example. This used to be a straightforward process of copyediting, image drawing, typesetting, printing, and distributing. Copyediting was often done by in-house staff; now the process is highly complex, with multiple outputs— print, online (XML, HTML, and PDF), app, metatdata, supplemental data, video, podcasts, and so on. Highly technical processes are used to ensure that a published article can be found and cited, including assigning and registering a unique DOI, creating the metadata and sending it out to multiple indexing agencies, tagging the content and indexing it for online searching, and creating and posting the app to the relevant app store. Although much of this work is outsourced to vendors in Asia, in-house staff is still needed to oversee the process. In addition, publishers employ many more technology staff, even if they use a vendor's hosting platform. Thus, in short, although the basic costs of production have been automated and offshored to reduce costs, the cost of supporting the hugely more complex technology is far higher than the savings.

Production costs are directly related to the number of pages that a journal publishes, whether for use only online or in print. The relentless increase in the total number of articles being submitted for publication inevitably puts pressure on a publisher to allow more pages for more content. Unless additional pages can be paid for by article processing charges from authors (whether hybrid options or full, open access, new launches) the overall price of the journal will need to be increased.

Another area that has seen a big change in costs is that of marketing. In the days of simple print subscriptions, marketers would produce print promotional pieces and mail them to potential customers. Customers could then respond directly to encourage their librarian to subscribe through a subscription agent. Marketing today entails gathering information about readers and usage to promote content to relevant people via online advertising and e-mail blasts. In addition, online content must be discoverable via search engines, so search engine optimization (SEO) is a new and important function in publishing, along with close monitoring of the usage of online sites. Marketing costs have therefore shifted from paying for print marketing pieces and distributing them to having technically competent, in-house teams to manage highly targeted campaigns. So any savings are simply taken up with new costs elsewhere.

The last cost that can be more of a challenge is the royalty return that is paid to societies. These tend to increase as a percentage of revenue and offering a guarantee is generally required to win the business.

So where does revenue come from? The majority of a journal's income generally comes from institutional subscriptions. The advertised institutional price does not indicate what the majority of customers might pay for access to a title. Most libraries will buy a bundle at a deep discount and often as part of a consortium of buyers, offering another level of discount. Growth in revenue generally comes from increasing the number of institutions worldwide that are buying bundles of journals. Although the price of a bundle will increase, sometimes ahead of the cost of living, this is generally a function of the number of pages being published and the increase in the overall cost base.

Journals also see income from the sale of individual articles, fees for permission to copy or use content, and reprint income from corporate customers who buy many copies of one article. Depending on the discipline, some journals may see individual subscriptions, and these may then attract a level of advertising, although steep declines in advertising have been reported in recent years. More recently journals have gained income from article processing fees, although this is generally a small portion of overall income.

With both income and costs under pressure, it is hard to balance the need for additional pages or issues to cope with the increase in content. This is the main job of the individual publisher managing a group of journals. A publisher needs to have a strategy to reduce costs where possible and a clear content publishing plan. This then gives a target of revenue to be achieved in order to maintain a balance and pay for any new content to be published.

If a surplus can be generated by careful management, this can then be reinvested in new, online hosting and tools/features to improve either services for authors or the online experience for readers. It may also be invested in launching new journals in new research areas, which rarely cover costs in the early years of publication.

Conclusion

While balancing and supporting the many and varied needs of different journal stakeholders can be a challenge, it is also very satisfying to see a good journal get even better, an editor feel a sense of achievement when the journal's impact factor increases, or a new companion journal can be launched. In the same way that a conductor can say that they helped the orchestra to perform magnificently without playing a note themselves, a publisher also helps the journal ecosystem to thrive in challenging times. This is a true partnership—without working with all stakeholders who all want a journal to succeed, a publisher would be like a conductor who has an orchestra with only violas! Without journals we would not have well-respected and widely read research that supports the careers of authors around the world. This is what makes a publisher get out of bed in the morning.

The Future

» In my opinion, journals will continue to provide a vital service in the communication of research for many years to come. I do not subscribe to the view often put forward that the days of journals are numbered.

» Open access or article processing charges are here to stay and provide some ability to fund the increase in volume of global research

» The rise of fraudulent services, content, and even journals is a major concern and one that needs to be tackled by all involved in journal publishing. This issue is not going to go away.

» Despite the fact that it is widely viewed that publishers add little or nothing to the creation of a journal, we will continue to bring talent and creativity to our journals in support of our authors, editors, and readers

ACKNOWLEDGMENTS: Many thanks to my colleagues at Wolters Kluwer for their comments on my chapter, but special thanks to Michelle Brewer. All commentary and opinions are my own and do not necessarily reflect the views of Wolters Kluwer.

Notes

1. "The Impact Factor" is calculated and published by Thomson Reuters, see http://wokinfo.com/essays/impact-factor for more information.

2. A 2015 study in *Science*, http://www.sciencemag.org/news/2015/06/study-claims-28-billion-year-spent-irreproducible-biomedical-research talks about this being a $28 billion problem, based on "past studies of error rates in biomedical studies."

3. PubMed Central® (PMC) is a free, full-text archive of biomedical and life sciences journal literature at the U.S. National Institutes of Health's National Library of Medicine (NIH/NLM)# published papers. http://www.ncbi.nlm.nih.gov/pmc (Accessed July 2016).

4. Kantar Media measures the readership of leading medical journals and provides information to potential advertisers, see http://www.kantarmedia.com/us/our-solutions/audience-measurement/readership-and-text.

—— 10 ——

ACQUISITIONS: WHERE DO BOOKS COME FROM?

Steven D. Smith, D.Phil.

////////////// TOP TAKEAWAYS IN THIS CHAPTER

» A strategic approach to acquisitions

» The primary responsibilities and skills of an acquisitions editor

» The main elements of a publishing plan

» Soliciting the proposal and managing expectations

» Acquisitions as a reactive and iterative process

» Different types of reviewing

» Basic elements of contracts and negotiating

» Benefits of development

Where do books come from? More generally, where does scholarly content come from? Quite simply, it is the role and responsibility of the acquisitions editor to sponsor, commission, or acquire books or scholarly content for their respective presses.

The Role of the Acquisitions Editor

At its best, this can be a kind of magical, intoxicating process, working in close quarters with authors, in the realm of ideas, to create a product of lasting scholarly value. Books can change lives, influence the way students learn a subject for years to come, or have an impact on public discourse. But it isn't

all about "big game hunting"—behind the apparent glamour, there is an organizational process, administrative rigor, strategic planning, implementation,
and execution, much of which must happen quickly, accurately, and at some
considerable volume.

At the same time, most books don't just "happen" as if by accident, or come
unsolicited. Rather, the projects are commissioned. An acquisitions editor
(AE) not only finds a project, they champion the project within the publishing
house, as it represents a serious financial investment.

In this chapter, we will go on a tour of the main elements of acquisitions, in
particular, the role of the AE, why it matters, the process, the skills, and how
it works in practice, in relation to the overall strategy of the publisher. For
purposes of this discussion, I suggest we don't get too hung up on the different types of books and commercial models of publishing, although I'll sketch
those out where pertinent. For purposes of the present discussion, unless otherwise indicated, let's focus on a scholarly book or monograph of some kind.

A Strategic Approach: Hunting Rather Than Fishing

The naive answer to the question "Where do books come from?" is that in our
ideal world books and manuscripts are simply written by authors, researchers,
professors, and scholars and sent directly to publishers for publication, and
that is the end to it. That is where books come from.

In this naive schema, all manuscripts and books are essentially "unsolicited" and the only possible role for the AE is that of a facilitator, an enthusiastic
administrator of sorts. Yes, there is some basic assessment of the manuscript,
with external reviewers, but otherwise the AE's role is to ensure that the project progresses through the publishing process as smoothly and efficiently as
possible. As sponsor of the project, the AE ensures that the project is brought
through the publisher's internal approval process in a timely manner. In so
doing, the AE works with colleagues to ensure that good decisions are made
about how best to publish the book in order to maximize its potential. The
AE ensures that information feeds accurately to external sources (like Amazon), facilitates communication between the author/editor and the publisher,
all while maintaining the book's schedule. All of this eventually results in a

finished product, namely, a published book. And if the naive view of "where books come from" were all there was to publishing, then we could pretty much end our chapter here.

Now, depending on the publisher, it *is* sometimes the case that a number of manuscripts or proposals do come unsolicited to an AE and of those, a certain percentage might end up being published. In these cases, the unsolicited manuscript or proposal might be for a work that is deemed to be outstanding and fits with what the AE happens to be seeking at that moment. This "fit" could be a matter of blind luck, but of course the odds can be reduced ahead of time if the author(s) has done their homework and determined that the project in question is a good strategic fit with the list or press in question. They might have done this in various ways. Perhaps they had the foresight to seek the AE out at a conference and ask pointed questions about their commissioning strategy, for example, "What kind of projects are you looking for?" Or perhaps they examined the publisher's own program of publishing and could see that their own manuscript would be a good fit with the strengths of this particular publisher. But for many publishers, this somewhat naive vision of books arriving unsolicited over the transom, fitting with the AE's overall commissioning strategy, is just that: a naive vision, and in itself does not represent a viable strategy.

What's more, many major publishers do not accept unsolicited proposals or manuscripts, due either to the poor quality of the submissions or because of the sheer volume of unsolicited proposals. AEs cannot wait for great projects to drop onto their desks out of the blue. Rather, they are paid to proactively search for new projects that are a good fit for the needs of their respective press.

With that in mind, an AE is expected to adopt a strategic approach to acquisitions. This requires having a vision and specific objectives for the program, a strategy for achieving these objectives, and an accompanying list of targets. Simply put, it means hunting rather than fishing. Much as an architect might have a vision for a building and then set about building it, an acquisitions editor should have a vision for a subject area and then set about implementing the plan systematically. What this means in practice is that the AE actively commissions key projects, or titles, in order to make good on his or her plan.

Just as an architect is not going to wait passively for random bricks and stones to arrive in order to build his or her edifice, similarly an acquisitions editor is not going to wait passively for random proposals and manuscripts to arrive over the transom to build a program.

What Are the Primary Responsibilities of an Acquisitions Editor?

In terms of acquiring content, the AE's responsibility is to develop a strategic vision for the program and, after agreeing on a list of targets with the editorial director and his or her respective publishing team, set about commissioning these projects (and new editions, where necessary) in order to make good on their plan. These must be the very best projects insofar as they fit with the strategic vision of the list, which in turn must fit with the overall strategy of the publisher in question. In other words, most AEs don't have carte blanche to acquire just any books: rather, the vision for the program must play to the overall strategic strengths of the press. But apart from acquiring content, what other role does the AE have in the scholarly publishing process?

The AE's responsibilities could simply begin and end with acquiring new content—be a "big game hunter," as it were. He or she could commission (sign) a big book project and walk away from it, meaning that everyone else in the team has to get on with the hard work of writing, developing, producing, marketing, and selling the work and rights on behalf of the author. But as the overall sponsor of a publishing program or list, the AE's responsibilities don't stop with signing a project because they have full oversight of the development of the overall program as well as the successful publication of individual books or projects (or what are sometimes called "products" in the digital era). Broadly speaking, this means overseeing and working as part of a team to develop and prepare manuscripts for transmittal to production. Publishing on this score is very much a team enterprise, and it's the AE's responsibility to provide full oversight of the project, from signature of the contract through to publication and beyond.

What this means in practical terms is twofold. Facing the external world, the AE must work with reviewers and authors of both new and previously contracted books to develop proposals, chapters, and manuscripts. Broadly speaking, the key with proposal or manuscript development is early intervention, that is, steering the author early in terms of the level, structure, coverage, length, strategy, contents, pedagogy, and so forth, in terms of its intended readership. The AE and author/editor need to be clear about what is referred to as a project's USP, or unique selling point.

Facing the world internal to the publisher, the AE must champion the work by liaising with colleagues in production regarding print and digital formats, design, and scheduling. The AE must also work closely with colleagues in marketing in terms of print runs, formats, prices, marketing plans, and preparation of publicity (such as book reviews). It might also mean presenting forthcoming titles to sales representatives.

In practical terms, it also means ensuring that all data (such as the title, book description, author description, endorsements, length, formats, prices, etc.) that feed to external sources such as catalogues, flyers, publicity, and websites such as Amazon, is full and accurate at all times. This latter bit is perhaps tedious but of critical importance. Get it wrong and external websites everywhere are populated with erroneous information.

In all this, the AE is responsible for the overall intellectual and fiscal health of their respective program. Even at smaller university presses and nonprofits, an AE will be expected to run their program with some modicum of basic fiscal management and financial oversight. The best scholarly publishing programs of course make an impact in their communities, but increasingly they are expected to pull their weight financially and to make a certain commercial contribution to the financial sustainability of the publisher as well. Certainly, in commercial publishing, the financial imperative is even more direct, sometimes with minimum financial requirements to do with revenue and profitability.

What Are the Primary Skills of an Acquisitions Editor?

There are three key primary skills for an AE to run his or her program. The first is list management; by this I mean achieving all key indicators, in particular (1) revenue, (2) signing targets, (3) the projects published in any given year, and (4) the number of manuscripts transmitted to production. It can also include any special objectives, such as signing a major reference work, an important new edition, or a key author.

The second key role is in terms of relationship management. The AE must develop a dynamic and ongoing relationship with authors, contributors, and key advisers. He or she must also collaborate with colleagues in other parts of the business, such as journals, marketing and sales, production, and finance in order to coordinate overall strategies and timely delivery of products that meet specifications, revenue, and profitability goals. It may mean liaising with journals colleagues to maintain and develop appropriate contacts with journals editors and societies. It may mean working closely with product development colleagues to develop digital formats, again, on time and on specification.

The third key role is in terms of project management. Here the AE must agree on overall project schedules and track deadlines in conjunction with editorial assistants, managing editors, development editors, production editors, and project editors, as required. They must work as part of a team to research, create, implement, and track projects including books, ancillaries, and electronic products. The AE must track project financials and maintain budgets and work as part of a team to increase project and overall profitability while lowering costs. Essentially, the AE must manage the "front list" (forward publishing stream) and "back list" (previously published titles).

The Role of the Acquisitions Editor

We have looked at the key responsibilities and skills of an acquisitions editor. What, then, is the role of an AE within the context of the life of a book?

The following are the three main elements of the AE's role:

>> Planning
>> Commissioning
>> Publishing

For purposes of this chapter, let's focus on planning and commissioning. If our AE is to go hunting rather than fishing, then it suggests directed and not aimless behavior. This focused action begins with planning, specifically, the research phase of commissioning.

There are many ways an AE can shape his or her commissioning plans. In a digital world, for example, he or she could use article usage to form a view about research interest or potential market. More commonly, the AE needs to build up a view of the market, size of the audience/readership, the curriculum (for textbooks), competition (such as competing titles, ancillaries, or in terms of other publisher) and work backward from there. The output of this research, analysis, strategy, and targets is a publishing plan.

What Are the Main Elements of a Publishing Plan?

1. *Strategic position.* This should set out a vision for the program. What is distinctive about the program in relation to its competitors? What is its trajectory and ambition? And, more specifically, what is the specific plan and timeline to achieve these goals? In all of this, the AE must set out this strategic position in relation to the press's overall business model and business strategy.

2. *Competition analysis.* As above, the AE must understand and be able to narrate their program's position relative to the constellation of key competitors. Here it is helpful to be able to conduct a so-called SWOT analysis (evaluation of the main strengths, weaknesses, opportunities, and threats.)

3. *Course map.* For books intended for courses, an AE could work backward from a course map, which includes the curriculum, the main competing texts, and the main previously published textbooks (listed under their respective course titles), with key acquisitions targets. A course map serves as a kind of litmus test for AEs in college publishing—simply put, all targets should exist under their intended courses. A course map also serves as an educational tool internally.

4. *Sales analysis.* An AE and their respective product (marketing) manager need to understand the sales performance of all titles, certainly key titles, and all recent titles—front list, recent back

list, and back list. What works, in what formats, in which regions, and why? What did not live up to expectations, and why not? In all of this, it is useful to focus on the "top 25" projects, both in the current year and in comparison with previous years, to see which lessons can be learned in terms of the types of books that are successful and what the decline or increase in rate of sales looks like.

5. *Road map.* For strategic publishing, AEs and their teams should create a "road map" of key indicators—namely, target versus actual in relation to revenue, signings, and publishing—looking at least three years backward and projecting three-years forward. This visual overview shows the trajectory of the program in terms of revenue, signings, and publishing. Is it growing or declining? What are the trends, and why?

6. *Strategies.* The key strategies provide a clear plan of action to achieve the overall objectives for the program. The strategy provides a coordinated approach to growth on the list, with a clear direction and focus on certain actions. The main headlines of such a plan might be as follows:

>> Focus on the key emerging themes in the subject area
>> Focus on advanced textbooks and reference projects in these subject areas
>> Invest in interdisciplinary areas
>> Focus on emerging markets in Asia
>> Maximize digital sales in the context of ongoing decline of print sales
>> Focus on disciplines where we have significant journals presence
>> Develop a series of projects
>> Strike a strategic partnership with a leading society in the field

Under each headline specific examples might follow. The goal in this particular case is to generate growth based on this approach. The overall plan summarizes the objectives and explains each of the key elements of the plan of action.

7.   *Key targets.* The strategic plan will include a list of key commissioning targets and perhaps a list of authors for those projects. This list of targets should be "owned" by the publishing team. The targets should focus acquisitions efforts. At the same time, the list is always evolving and should be updated constantly by the AE. It should be revisited and revised on a regular basis in response to questions such as, Which key targets have been signed? Has the market changed? Has a new competitor appeared on the market? And so forth.

In summary, the publishing plan in its entirety sets out an AE's vision and ambition for the list and should serve as a kind of narrative as to where they and the publishing team are going. It can energize colleagues internally and the academic community, externally. But it can also serve as a flash point: Is everyone in agreement about the vision, and strategy? Is everyone in agreement about key targets? If not, now is the time to work out differences.

With a strategic plan in place, the AE can systematically set about commissioning their key targets. But how?

Commissioning Key Targets

We have now come to the nub of the question: Where does scholarly content come from? With their publishing plan in place, the AE can begin to implement their plan and acquire their main targets. Following this top-down approach, the AE must identify potential authors for these projects—at least where the list of targets does not also include an author whom they would want for that project. An AE has many ways of doing this:

» Asking authors they trust
» Doing their own research
» Reading journals
» Poaching from other publishers
» Looking at entries in reference books
» And, crucially, building their own networks

Editor networks are built by visiting campuses, attending conferences, via telephone calls, talking to reviewers, via e-mail, and so forth. In the process, the AE can build up a short list of potential candidates for their target project(s) and work backward from there. Essentially the AE is trying to be a matchmaker of sorts—matching a specific author with a specific project.

Approaching an Author: Persuasion and Timing

Persuading an author is all about knowing the kind of project that might motivate them. But it's also about timing—finding and approaching the right person at the right time with a compelling idea. For example, an AE might know of a great author who has just finished a particular assignment or project for a very small specialist readership. Perhaps this is good time to initiate a discussion about an academic trade or textbook.

Is there anything to prevent the author from running off with the idea to another publisher? In a sense, very little. It happens, but not very often. If the AE approaches the author with an idea, he or she has some moral claim over the project and will, in practice, rarely lose a project to another publisher in this manner.

In all of this, the AE needs to be conscious that they are bringing value to the author—namely, their professional expertise, judgment, creativity, knowledge of the market, assessment of the opportunity, as well as their clout within the press, that is, their ability to get things done such as negotiating good terms, getting a flyer, a book launch, a four-color cover, ensuring attendance at the right conferences, arranging publicity, and so forth.

The enthusiasm an AE shows for a project can set the tone for the rest of the relationship and is hopefully reciprocated. If there is little enthusiasm on the part of the author at this early stage, this may be a sign of difficulties to come when it comes to the business of writing and adhering to a schedule. It may, in fact, indicate that the project may never be completed—as many as 10 percent of projects under contract never get written. There are many conflicting priorities in the life of an academic.

However, the AE must also take care to manage expectations. The risk here is that the AE's initial enthusiasm traps them into making unreasonable promises to the author. Of course, savvy authors may try to use this enthusiasm as leverage to extract further financial demands. The key for an AE is to be clear and forthright about what they can and cannot deliver in terms of finances, development, production, marketing, conferences, and so forth; and to be clear at least in their own mind (and with their editorial director) about what they are (and are not) willing to spend for a project.

Persuasion is itself a double-edged sword. An AE's charismatic ability to persuade a key author to undertake a major project can be impressive and intoxicating, but ultimately it will be a Pyrrhic victory if the project is never written. Persuading someone against their better judgment inevitably leads to a pipeline of projects that are unlikely ever to be written. By and large, the AE wants to locate an author who shares their enthusiasm and sense of urgency for the project.

Why should an author publish with one particular AE rather than anyone else? Above all, it will be about the relationship the author has with an AE. But the AE needs to be clear about what they have to offer as a publisher. Why should an author publish with you rather than someone else? It will largely be about what the AE has to offer, their expertise, authority, credibility, enthusiasm, trust, and reputation (and people *do talk!*).

Of course, indirectly, it is also about their press's reputation and capabilities and about what it has to offer. An AE or press's reputation can often count for a lot. The upshot is that a big advance from a large publisher does not necessarily mean that a smaller advance from a reputable boutique press does not stand a chance. The brand of the smaller Ppress may hold sway. The AE from the smaller press may also have a stronger relationship with the author, or take the time to craft a proposal tailored specifically for the project in question, which, taken together, provides a more compelling offer.

The Proposal

How are great books commissioned? On many occasions, it is the result of an AE just remembering to ask! But there are different ways of asking (e.g., either directly or indirectly). AEs often approach a potential author, either my e-mail or by phone or in person (e.g., at a conference or during a campus visit) and simply raise the idea of a particular project, and take soundings as to an academic's potential interest in the project. Authors are not always ready to take a project on immediately; he or she may have other priorities and a long (sometimes *very* long) gestation period ensues. This is where the process of commissioning can be likened to a long-term conversation or discourse, through a relationship, re-established via meetings at conferences, and through regular contact, such as e-mail and other means of communication.

Given the opportunity cost associated with a project, it can be difficult for AEs to know when to give up on one author and move on. For a particularly important and valuable project, they may feel they can only wait for an answer from an author for so long. However, for present purposes, let's assume the AE has done their planning and has found an author who is keen on the idea and responds in a reasonable amount of time. They have agreed to sketch out an initial proposal for the project. And if the author is an academic, at least in theory, they have an intrinsic motivation to publish.

At the very least, a book proposal should contain a title; rationale; envisaged list of contents; comment on the market, readership, competition (competing books); along with a brief biographical statement, just to get the ball rolling. But how does an AE get the author to write the initial book proposal? Sometimes with great difficulty! AEs have been known to plead, beg, cajole, and bribe, all to little avail. In fact, AEs have also been known to write a rough draft of the proposal themselves to chivvy the process along, or to use a copy of the course syllabus as the basis of a proposal (in the case of a textbook).

If there can be this much difficulty getting a proposal for a book, what about obtaining a draft chapter or manuscript further down the road? There are indeed various obstacles in the way between the author as academic and the manuscript project. Arguably, the main hurdle here is the notion of the "overburdened academic." In this view, there are competing demands on the time and energy of lecturers and increased disincentives to write the kinds of books some publishers want.

The second theme is competitor pressure. The likelihood is that the AE is at a scholarly press, perhaps competing with a big trade publisher or college publisher for the time and attention of a key author. For example, if you're a psychology author, your publishing choices are as follows: publish original research in journal articles for career advancement; publish with a big trade publisher for fame and a large advance; or publish a textbook with a big college publisher for a large sum of money.

Where does that leave the small scholarly publisher? One response for the smaller boutique press might be to retreat into more specialized niches, in terms of subject areas, or to be more responsive in terms of digital formats to be more nimble and provide a better product and service to authors and customers.

In the meantime, the upshot is that there is even less time to write books and an enhanced disconnect between books for professional advancement and the kinds of books publishers can profitably publish. In addition, there are other hurdles specific to some disciplines, such as the life sciences—running a lab, grant applications, and the competing attractions of clinical work, consulting, and so forth.

In sum, even when an AE can persuade an author to write a book, there is no guarantee the author will deliver a manuscript in a timely maner. Writing the manuscript can sink to the bottom of an ever-increasing in-box of teaching, admin, committee work, research, grading, and so forth.

Reviewing the Proposal

There are different ways of reviewing a proposal—in particular, "wide and shallow" versus "deep and narrow." The former can consist of an online survey, the latter a smaller number of in-depth specialized reviews. Most importantly, the AE needs to ask the right questions. For example, of a textbook, "Would you adopt this book?" Responses can be very telling.

In assessing the proposal, the AE needs to be clear about what is distinctive about the book or project in question. In addition, how well does the proposal map onto the AE's vision for the book? And how well does this project map onto the strategic strengths of the publisher?

In many ways, this is where the proverbial magic happens in the commissioning process—the creative exchange between an editor and an author, in relation to the reviewers.

Contracts and Negotiating

Negotiating a successful agreement sometimes means knowing when it is possible to give in, or split the difference over something, to give on one point (such as an improved escalator on the royalties) in order to obtain something in return (a faster delivery date for the manuscript), and so forth.

After a project has been formally approved according to the press's internal approval processes, the AE will make any necessary changes from the publishing group meeting notes and submit the proposal in internal publishing systems. The AE will then contact the authors/editor with the contract terms. Once all parties have agreed, the AE drafts the contract. After authors have returned their fully signed contracts, it is important to promptly establish contact and start them off on the right foot. At this point, AEs usually e-mail authors with information custom-tailored to their project and talk about development, the schedule, formatting, submission guidelines, etc.

Development

Development helps publishers manage the risk inherent in higher investment projects by controlling the quality of their textbook output. The term *development* covers the interventions a book undergoes to ensure it will compete aggressively in the relevant market, thus increasing adoptions and revenue. This is achieved in development by making sure that the textbook meets and exceeds the standards set by existing competing texts in its overall approach, its coverage, tone and style, pedagogy, design, and presentation.

The benefits of development can be summarized as follows:

>> Risk reduction. Often, markets are crowded and highly competitive— early and thorough research into the relevant courses and the competing titles (including their online resources) not only ensures the right project is being endorsed but also helps set the focus for the project's progression.

>> Confident publishing. Taking a closer look at chapter content and layout early on allows publishers to catch errors in coverage, tone, style, and pedagogy and to control the overall approach of the project.

>> Clear, unique selling points. Development can be critical in identifying the niche in the market their book will fill, and ensuring that the final text has a clear, attractive unique selling point (USP).

>> Useful commissioning tool. Development can be viewed as a service offered by editorial departments, which can be promoted as a benefit of working with a particular AE as a textbook author.

>> Greater accountability. Development can help engage authors and encourage their adherence to a planned delivery schedule.

>> Cohesive learning packages. Researching competing online resources and discussing them with the author at the very beginning allows time to establish what needs to be done to satisfy (and exceed) the market requirements in the area.

>> Collaboration and communication. Authors have clear expectations of the textbook writing process and feel supported in their efforts with ongoing feedback and communication from editorial staff through-out the writing process. Equally, knowledge is shared throughout the in-house team, enabling editorial, marketing, and production to make informed choices that support the goals and projected market position of the book.

Agreeing on a manuscript development plan with an author from the onset is crucial. The AE need not be apologetic nor defensive about any of this. Most authors appreciate efforts that help make their work better and maximize the developmental process. The key is to involve the author in the process and provide for early reviews of the first few chapters. The most effective time in developmental reviewing is early on in the writing process, when authors are able and receptive to changing key elements such as level, style, or structure. The AE or developmental editor should also be prepared to follow up with the author on a regular basis throughout the writing process. In all of this, the developmental efforts and investment should be scaled accordingly in terms of time and money. Not all books warrant development, or certainly not the same amount of development. For example, the effort put behind a massive intro college textbook is of a different order than what might be undertaken for something that will be used in a graduate seminar.

Development should be an integral part of the editorial process from day one. A development editor can ensure the legitimacy and safety of larger investments and the quality of publishing output. They make sure key textbooks receive the editorial attention they need and can also, in this way, assist in managing the workload that accompanies weightier book projects. Larger-scale development is a vital resource for any academic publisher serious about producing quality, successful textbook packages. But scaled appropriately, manuscript development is a kind of investment that can be applied to all book projects to reduce risk and improve rates of success.

Conclusion

Books and new products come from the AE's strategic approach to acquisitions. The AE is responsible for articulating a strategic vision for their program in a competitive and fast-changing environment. They need to identify and sign key projects and authors for their respective lists and, within their team context, oversee the successful development and publication of all projects to ensure the program achieves agreed targets for, say, overall list revenue and indicative number of projects.

On a microlevel, the AE is the sponsor for each project. But at a macrolevel, they are the steward for their program, and in this respect their overriding responsibility is to the press and maintaining the financial health of the list. These should be complementary roles, since it is in everyone's interest for each book to do well and for the overall program to remain viable. Effective publishing means that the AE must develop a collaborative publishing team, that is, he or she must work closely and effectively with editorial, production, and marketing colleagues throughout the editorial and publishing process to ensure coordinated overall strategies and timely deliveries of books to maximize business objectives. But the AE also needs to think of their relationship with an author over the long term—beyond one or more books, and of course some books will go into multiple editions over the course of many years, perhaps through the duration of an entire career. That is, the AE needs to develop and maintain positive and productive lifelong network of contacts with authors, contributors, and key advisers.

While I have described a strategic approach to acquisitions, what gets left out in all of this is the magic of working in the realm of ideas. There is a genuine give and take, a creative exchange that happens in discussions with authors during which what might start out as one thing ends up as another, morphing and evolving along the way, sometimes in unpredictable ways. The AE can serve as a catalyst in this process, and this is what can make publishing itself so profoundly gratifying—the realization that the book itself exists because it was commissioned, and ultimately became what it is because of the AEs interventions along the way: perhaps its coverage, level and content, and its overall shape all are the result of a creative process.

Publishing is itself undergoing enormous and constant change due to the evolution of print-to-digital formats, new business models, new products, constant cost-cutting, with outsourcing and offshoring, as well as growth and decline in regional markets, and of course massive challenges and opportunities presented by the rise of social media, open access, and open education resources (OER). At the same time, there has never been a more exciting time to create new, dynamic digital products, going beyond the traditional book. Acquisitions is enormously challenging, stimulating, thrilling, rewarding, and gratifying, particularly if the books and digital products are well received by the community.

The Future

The role of acquisitions will continue to evolve as publishing is subject to continuous disruptive innovations:

>> Those in acquisitions need to look beyond traditional formats (such as monographs) to more innovative digital formats and platforms as publishing itself continues to evolve. This may mean collaborating with different stakeholders across organizations, working with digital product developers, creating new business models, and developing hybrid programs.

>> The decline of traditional publishing formats and other developments threatens to disrupt or disintermediate publishers, or make them seem

anachronistic. The challenge is to reposition and reinvent ourselves to thrive in a world in which technology and social networking ultimately transform the way end users and communities develop and use content.

» Publishers must also adapt to the opportunity of open access and open educational resources. We must find scalable and sustainable approaches to open publishing and archiving and lead in the development of digital scholarship and support the dissemination of knowledge.

» Publishers must manage the transition from print to digital. If print is increasingly a commodity, the self-funding press must find ways to add value by investing in digital infrastructure, formats, and services while streamlining workflows and reducing costs.

Further Readings

Davies, Gil. *Book Commissioning and Acquisition*, 2nd ed. Abingdon, UK: Routledge, 2004.

John Thompson. *Merchants of Culture: The Publishing Business in the Twenty-First Century*. Cambridge, UK: Polity Press, 2012.

11

FINDING A NEEDLE IN A HAYSTACK: THE SAGA OF A REFERENCE BOOK

Rolf A. Janke

////////////// TOP TAKEAWAYS IN THIS CHAPTER

» The transitions from print to digital reference

» Building a "must-have" reference work

» What not to publish

» Past, present, and future thoughts on Wikipedia

» Why reference titles still matter

» Is there a future for reference?

The year is 2001. Most academic libraries hailed their reference section as the go-to place for finding a solution to the patron's research needs. The reference section . . . you know, the big room with stacks and stacks of single volume and multivolume reference works on almost every topic of relevance and of importance to the entire campus community. It was the place where you could find the answer to almost any question you have. Fast-forward to present day, 2016. That glorious room is now a café, or perhaps an information commons, where students gather, chat, collaborate, learn, or just hang out. Computer screens buzz with Google and Wikipedia searches, which produce endless results of information, which can produce a most inquisitive frown on a student's face, wondering if the results of the search are accurate, or even more importantly, allowed to be cited in his or her paper. Perhaps an overstated comparison, but in 2001 a quick search in a printed reference book produced authoritative results, and now, finding that type of result can be viewed the same as finding a needle in a haystack.

The emergence of digital content, aggregated databases, the free World Wide Web—just to name a few variables—have all led to the concept of discoverability. How do I find something I didn't know that I didn't know? Before we answer that question, we must consider a very important component of the entire reference ecosystem. I am speaking of the content creator of reference, the publisher.

The academic publishers who create the reference content have seen a steady decline in sales; the haystack is still there, it's just not filled with as many needles. This economic loss has driven some publishers to go out of business, cease publishing reference, or scale back so significantly that their reference division is a small part of a bigger entity within that publisher. The saga of the reference book has been playing out for several years and I am afraid will continue to do so for more to come. It's a matter of supply and demand for current reference publishers, which dictates the economic outcome of their program, and in every editorial boardroom, there is a survival guide for staying in business. In this chapter, I will explore the risks and rewards of a sustainable reference program, but first we need to put how we got here into historical perspective.

Print Rules (or It Used to . . .)

For many decades leading into the early 21st century, reference publishers had a sound editorial model backed by customer demand for subject-specific encyclopedias, atlases, dictionaries, and handbooks. These products came in many shapes and sizes but their common denominator was that they were printed books. Before the Internet, these books were in big demand by librarians, and back in the day, there probably wasn't enough floor space for all the stacks of shelves to house wonderful titles such as *The Encyclopedia of the Cold War* to the *Dictionary of Molecular Biology* to the *Atlas of the Americas*. Their purpose was to give a student a sense of direction, both general or specific, about even the narrowest of topics. At the end of the day, a book was published by a company, bought by a library, used by a student; repeat. Academic reference publishers built their editorial, sales, and marketing infrastructure around the good economic times when print sales were healthy. It should be mentioned that the investment in such was large scale—the creation of authoritative, printed materials did come at a cost. Sustainability was based on how many books you produced at the lowest cost with the most sales.

Reference books by design were a research tool for the entire campus community but mostly served an undergraduate audience. Academic journals and monographs served the graduate and faculty research needs. Interestingly, academic journals and reference works had something very much in common that had nothing to do with their intended audience or pricing model: both were filled with chunks of information. Chunks, defined, were small-, medium-, or large-sized articles. These products were not necessarily cover-to-cover reads. They were "get in, get what you need, and get out" research tools. This is a very important factor to what happened next in the evolution of the reference work.

As digital technology and the Internet improved at nanosecond speeds in the 1990s, publishers of academic journals saw great opportunities in taking their content online. Remember, a single journal issue is a collection of articles, each one written to stand alone. Thus, journal publishers either built their own digital platforms or aggregated their content with another company—either way, libraries lined up to purchase the digital content as it made not only perfect sense for the publishers to move in this direction, it made even better sense for the library. This new paradigm shift did not make the printed journal issues extinct, but it was an exciting time to see new content and business models get widely adapted in the higher education environment.

Meanwhile, printed reference continued to thrive as we moved into the 21st century, but it became very hard to ignore what was happening to the digital realm of the journal. The big question for the reference publisher was, you built your infrastructure (editorial, production, sales, marketing) around print—what do you now need to add to incorporate a digital strategy? Seems like an easy solution to work out—just ask the journal folks. Actually, it wasn't that easy at all. The editorial models are somewhat similar, but fast-forward to the business model: much different. Journals are sold through subscription pricing and reference works are sold as stand-alones.

It could be stated that journals were far more profitable because of their subscription nature, thus allowing for a greater investment risk toward building a digital strategy. So, back to the question posed for the reference field. How do you move forward toward putting your content online? Again, what do you add? This is the perfect time to fast-forward to present day as the question that should have been asked back then is the same as today—not what you should add to a reference work but what you should delete. But hindsight is always 20/20, right?

Absorb, Adapt, Embrace

As e-books became more popular, so did the desire and need for what I will call e-reference. Publishers had to absorb all the e-book technologies and business models. They needed to absorb the emergence of the ebook aggregators and what their roles were. But most importantly they needed to absorb how the libraries themselves were transitioning and learning about e-books.

Once reference publishers absorbed the emerging e-book ecosystems, it was time to adapt. Publishers had to figure out a myriad of items, some familiar, some not so familiar. The familiar included publishing the ever-so-familiar printed book. One of the things they gleaned from the libraries in transition is that they were still buying print, even if they were starting to buy e-reference. On the not-so-familiar, a huge fork in the road to sustainability appeared before them. In one direction, should they build their own platforms to host their digitized reference content or should they license all their content to an e-book aggregator, such as Gale Virtual Reference, Credo Reference, and myilibrary, to name just a few. Or, should they take both paths?

Finally, the publishers needed to realize that whatever they absorbed, whichever fork in the road they turned on, they simply needed to embrace that reference publishing had entered into a new era and that long-term sustainability was an issue. As time went on, print sales declined and publishers had to embrace that. On the other hand, e-reference sales were increasing but from a starting point of zero, so in some cases the results were a bit misleading. That scenario had to be embraced as well.

During this transition from print to digital, it was time to move the revenue needle from a single book via single purchase to selling collections of books. These collections came in all shapes and sizes; some were in a subject-specific collection, some were the publisher's entire catalog. Developing an e-reference collection was an easy proposition if you had all of your content digitized. I call this the "big check" process, where reference publishers could sell frontlist, backlist, subject-specific collections that meant the cost to the library was far greater than if they were just picking up a few books here or there. This made for interesting times for reference publishers as they viewed selling big collections as a way to resuscitate their declining revenues. It worked, on paper. But the issue moving forward was that feeding your platform, or aggregators, year after year with vast quantities of books just wasn't sustainable. For example, when a reference publisher introduces their launch collections (assume the frontlist collection contains 25 titles and the backlist collection contains 250), libraries are excited to buy both, especially if you are a publisher that specializes in a certain discipline like medicine or social sciences. Move to the next year and the publisher rolls out their new frontlist collection. In response to overall economic factors, the publisher scaled back on new product—the frontlist is now only 18 titles. The next year maybe 12. As you can see, the concept of building collections perhaps was more of a static than a fluid proposal. Mind you, certain publishers have such rich, deep backlists that they can mine those and create subcollections or have enough critical mass that revenue streams are more robust.

"Must Have" Versus "I Wish I Could Have"

As a reference publisher, I was caught up in the e-reference boom and it was my top priority to make sure content was available on as many platforms as possible. I guess you could say publishers figured out that taking both forks in the road was the most desirable strategy to be profitable. However, something that became evident 10 years ago is still very much the mind-set at libraries today; a title is published in whatever format, on whatever topic, and at whatever price, but it comes down to staff at the library asking, "Is this a 'must-have' book?" Criteria that perhaps define the "must-haves" would be the following:

» Faculty request

» Interdisciplinary, can be used by several departments

» Price

» Ties to a particular curriculum

» Authoritative

» Publisher known for quality publications

» Award-winning

Or librarians were saying, "Great book, I wish we could have it in our collection but limited resources will prevent us from purchasing it." One of the most significant aspects of reference collection development is that as a library, you really only need one definitive source on a topic. If there are two encyclopedias on the same topic, from a budget point of view, librarians would only buy one. There has to be some significant editorial homework done by the publisher to print a work that is both original and considered a must-have.

CASE STUDY: THE ANATOMY OF PUBLISHING A "MUST-HAVE"

The following case study is based on real events at Mission Bell Media, a new publishing company with a publishing focus on leadership studies content, and the publisher of this book.

The company increases its market research to focus on publishing interdisciplinary, cutting-edge and relevant topics that can be tied to respective curriculums. On Mission Bell Media's radar is the topic of African American leadership. It's certainly interdisciplinary and an extremely important and timely topic in today's political, social, and cultural climate.

The next step is to research whether there is any competition. There are several reference works on leadership and several on African American topics but not together as a single source. A quick canvass of this topic with a librarian advisory board yields a majority opinion of "thumbs up." The editorial team then moves on to the very challenging process of selecting a well-known academic scholar who can act as general editor for the project and lead a team of over 100 academics. Once the general editor is selected, it's important to define the scope and length of the work. The publisher takes into account that even though there could be enough content to fill two or three volumes, which would raise the retail price of the work, it decides under the must-have mindset to focus on a single-volume work, keeping the price attractive to librarians, not only for the reference section, but perhaps even for the circulating sections as well.

The general editor selected, in this case, is Tyson King-Meadows from the University of Maryland Baltimore County. Dr. King-Meadows is a distinguished scholar and has done a significant amount of research in the area of African American leadership. Another challenging task is selecting contributors to write the articles, carefully selected by the general editor, that will make up the work. It is very important to remember that in order for this work to be considered authoritative, the article contributors must be not only academics but experts in their respective disciplines. The issue here is that it has become extremely difficult in current times to convince an academic to write a 1,500- to 2,000-word article with the many other research priorities on his or her plate. Once all of the contributors are selected, the race against time begins. We are now probably one year into the project, and in order to publish a current resource, the publisher has to keep its radar on: one general editor, 125-plus contributors, and a promised publication date, which the editorial, development, and production teams have ingrained in their memory banks.

At this time, the publisher also reviews which cost-effective elements can add value to the work. There are so many components to be considered, some essential and obvious like a strong index and bibliography, but what about biographical essays, chronologies, videos for the digital version, images, and so on. All of these come at a cost and that cost is eventually passed on to the customer. I believe that part of the development of the must-have is ultimately the price. Keeping the bottom line in mind, it is decided that the index and bibliographies for *African American Leadership* will be the highest quality, with no added frills that would inflate the price. The publisher is now thinking what the review media might say—"The work could have benefited from biographical essays," or "This work could easily have been expanded into two volumes as there are so many topics not covered yet of significance for this topic." The publisher, quite honestly, is always thinking of what the review media will say—it's the nature of the business. But keeping in mind that the formula of producing relevant, authoritative content at an affordable price, delivered in multiple formats will more times than not garner a good review, and a reviewer just might say "It's a must-have."

While the book is in its final stages of development, the publisher zeros in on the marketing and sales plans. This includes strategies for both print and digital formats. Now comes the delicate process where the publisher looks at all the costs for the work—past, present, and future—and weighs those against the forecast of how many copies it will sell over, let's say, a two-year period. How many units of *African American Leadership* will sell in print? How many e-book aggregators will have access to the digital version via licensing agreements? How many will they sell? Suddenly, the profit-and-loss spreadsheet for this title just continued to page two. That first enthusiastic conversation with Dr. King-Meadows about taking on the project seems a distant memory, one now buried in the myriad of the economics of producing a profitable yet meaningful reference title. But then the magic happens! The articles are polished, then put through production, and the book starts looking like a book. Two years after the project began, the book makes its way out into the world—a single-volume reference work on a topic that librarians seem to agree is a must-have, as they find room in their budgets and collections to add a resource that will someday, hopefully, prove to be a valuable resource to a patron.

Although this is a condensed version of how this book came about, it is used here simply to illustrate that there are many pieces and parts to making a reference book and the challenges of making a book a must-have. It should also be stated that producing a must-have work is a subjective process. Who is the one ultimately deeming something a must-have? The publisher? The customer? The patron? I would expect that if all of these parties unanimously agree that it's a must-have, then maybe it is.

What Not to Publish

What wasn't stated in the case study are some of the realities of what not to publish. The following list provides examples of some of the types of books that publishers aren't including in their current editorial strategies. I believe that there are sound economic reasons behind each one, and it should be mentioned that this is not a definitive list for every publisher:

>> *New editions* (unless you are a science or medical publisher). New editions are a wild card in the reference business. The bottom line is that if libraries have limited budgets, they might find it hard to buy a new edition of something they already own. There are, of course, many exceptions to this rule, but if you are a social science or humanities publisher, you will need to do a great deal of due diligence on the first edition to decide whether or not to publish a second.

>> *Multivolume works.* Multivolume works are and will be a norm in reference publishing. But let's consider the price of a three-, four-, or more volume work. Publishers need to do some careful planning on when and if they publish multi-volume works, in the sense that you would not want to publish too many in one year. There is only so much money to go around.

>> *More than one work on the same topic.* Very few publishers take this on, but publishing more than one work on the same topic, even if slightly different, is not an economically sound idea. It is very tempting for publishers to do as one would want to franchise a hot topic, with multiple works coming at it from different angles, but as mentioned before—only so much money. Oh, and you are probably thinking maybe a multivolume might be the solution here. Please see the reason above.

>> *A work on a topic that has already been successfully published by a competitor.* One of the biggest challenges in list planning (the editorial process where publishers plan out, years in advance, what they want to publish and when) is not knowing what your competition has under development. Every once in a while, there is a topic or subject that everyone races to publish a work in. But as it turns out, the first one published usually wins, meaning that it will become a greater financial success than its followers. This is not to say that the followers are not good products, but libraries only have so much money and not knowing that more works are to come, they will buy the first one out.

>> *Biographical works.* The last item on my list comes from the result of many years of editorial research and the effects of the open Web. In years past, many publishers published biographical reference works or added a significant number of biographical essays to their products. This was a staple part of their development program. But as the Web and, more specifically, Wikipedia became a first stop for student research, finding biographical information on anyone—and I mean anyone—is quite easy. Not to water down the significance of biographical information, but odds are that that information is far more accurate on a free site than a topic that is more narrow yet requires a specific scholarly approach to define it.

As mentioned earlier, all of these products on my list are up for debate, not only among publishers, but with librarians as well. One would also ask, what's left to publish, based on my criteria. Remember, choose projects wisely as there is only so much money to go around.

Why Wikipedia Is a Good Thing

Moving on now to one of the ongoing debates that always loom large in editorial boardrooms is the world of Wikipedia and its impact on publishers, librarians, faculty, and patrons. Stating the obvious, this elephant has been in the room a very long time and everyone knows it's not moving anytime soon. Publishers were hit hard when Wikipedia emerged, and the effect probably did have a factor on lost revenue, albeit very hard to prove economically. Librarians were wary of Wikipedia at first, faculty as well. In reality, patrons were all smiles at the instant gratification of getting whatever they needed on literally every topic known to man in just seconds. Publishers tried to fight this with campaigns to promote their authoritative content over content that has been prepared by "who-knows-who," but to no avail. I believe that the timing of Wikipedia couldn't have been worse because as publishers grasped the total effects of what Wikipedia might bring, their print sales were in decline as well. The lost revenue effect from both sides presented some very difficult times for publishers, and something had to change. Publishers still had a structure in place to create, develop, and produce content; they just had accepted that Wikipedia was a preferred research tool, and yet despite this, there was still a place and need for the content publishers produced. In recent years I believe publishers finally saw the forest for the trees and figured out that after all of this consternation over this giant, the legacy of their brand and their products were still standing. Perhaps Wikipedia is a good thing after all? Of course it is. I am speaking now in contemporary terms but Wikipedia created a super-information highway for research and knowledge on the Web. But as reference publishers digitized their content and made it available through many different sources, librarians could offer authoritative solutions or even alternate points of view to Wikipedia to patrons, so even though Wikipedia remained the standard, the alternatives were most acceptable as well. So, publishers have come full circle since the birth of Wikipedia, and I am pleased to say that the chatter in the editorial boardrooms is that of brainstorming innovation and not predicting doomsday scenarios.

Many feel as information grows exponentially on the Web by the second, Wikipedia will lose its impact. This will become a real opportunity for publishers to create knowledge sources that marry good content with good formats and that through effective partnerships with libraries, can be discoverable. I am not sure we would have gotten to this point this quickly if it weren't for Wikipedia; thus Wikipedia really is a good thing.

Conclusion

First of all, let's remember that print reference is not dead and students still require sources of knowledge to assist in their research process. Somewhere in the middle of that, there lies the role of reference. Sure, libraries are weeding out reference sections and faculty may not be as endorsing as they once were, but it will all come down to value and format. Publishers have figured out, for the most part, the format component, but creating content that has value is going to remain the biggest challenge moving forward. Specifically, publishers want to be innovative yet need to be conservative on costs, which will have a direct impact on the reference content they want and/or need to create. It becomes quality over quantity packaged in a variety of formats delivered to a customer base that has little money to spend in the first place.

Very few reference publishers want to predict the future of where reference will be five or 10 years from now but they would predict that they'll still be creating content that serves a purpose. Libraries will always be at the ready for good reference content, which means that publishers need to work closely with them to make it easier for patrons to find those needles in the haystack. Once they do, all will be rewarded.

The Future of Reference Publishing

» Reference publishers will no longer use "encyclopedia" in their titles
» Reference publishers will experiment with business models for open-access reference
» Reference publishers will create online tools that will help integrate their reference content with course management tools such as Blackboard

───── 12 ─────

E-BOOKS ARE STILL BOOKS, AFTER ALL: THE CHALLENGE OF E-BOOK PUBLISHING AND CHANGING MODELS

Rebecca Seger

///////////// TOP TAKEAWAYS IN THIS CHAPTER

» Changing e-book business models are creating tremendous disruption for both libraries and publishers

» Monographs are costly to produce—that doesn't go away in a digital environment (and, in fact, the cost increases)

» E-Monographs offer a tremendous opportunity to discover the content in monographs previously locked in the printed book container on a shelf

» Publishers and libraries need to work together to continue experimenting on models that sustain a vital form of scholarly communication

Monograph: A detailed written study of a single specialized subject or an aspect of it.[1]

We are living in an era in which the advent of digital *everything* is producing enormous disruption in many areas of our lives—just look at what Amazon is doing to retail stores, what Uber is doing to taxis, and what business models are doing to traditional book purchases. E-books in libraries, particularly for academic use, are not immune to this disruption.

Sure, e-books in libraries have been around for nearly 20 years, with the first venture of note being netLibrary, founded in 1998. Since the early 2010s, however, there has been an explosion in the number of options for how to purchase e-books in academic libraries. We've got DDA (demand-driven acquisition), STL (short-term loan), EBA (evidence-based-acquisition), Access to Own, all in addition to collections models and title level purchasing that have been around far longer. Supporting all these new business models impacts everyone involved in actually getting books into libraries—publisher, library, suppliers, and lest we forget a very important part of the equation—authors. These impacts need to be appreciated and better understood by all involved.

The more publishers understand the library acquisition and selection process, and how and why budget issues force libraries to make hard decisions about book purchasing, the better publishers can avoid making uninformed decisions that create obstacles to purchasing and use. The more libraries understand the economics of publishing and how these new models impact publishers of very diverse types of books, the less confusing the decisions made by publishers can be to them. This chapter will aim to give more context to the publishing side of books and explain more openly the economics of book publishing so that staff at libraries will understand why there isn't a one-size-fits-all approach in e-book purchasing models.

Open Dialogue

As a publisher, and one who speaks to academic librarians and tries exceptionally hard to understand the point of view of libraries and end users (especially in relation to e-books), I believe in candor—in open, honest dialogue and sharing information about the economics of book publishing in a way that didn't need to be done in the print book-publishing world. In that much more simple world, a library bought a print book from the supplier of their choice (and there were many, perhaps hundreds), put it on the shelf, and didn't need to understand what else happened with the book outside the library walls—it had no bearing on the library's ability to purchase a copy. It could be a textbook, a monograph, a general interest nonfiction book, a fiction book, a book of poetry, an introductory book, a graduate-level textbook, a 100-page book, or a 1,000-page book. You knew what you were getting and publishers knew what you were doing with it. You could lend it when you wanted, loan it for an extended period to a faculty member, ILL (interlibrary loan) it to another university, and so on. There didn't need to be any conversation with the publisher about *how* it was used. The relationship between publisher and library ended there. Simple, right? Well, yes, it was. But what was really invisible to libraries was the vast diversity of the economic profiles of the books they were buying. Some of these books sold 100 copies. Some sold 100,000 copies. Some were purchased almost exclusively by libraries. Others had sales of maybe 5 percent to libraries, and 95 percent to a diverse consumer market, including to resellers, with Amazon accounting for up to 50 percent of that retail purchase. Others may have had a profile of maybe 10 percent bought by libraries, 30 percent bought by retail, and 60 percent purchased for courses (and not your standard pedagogical textbook).

Book Publishing Is a Risky Business

One of the least understood and perhaps least talked-about aspects of publishing is the much riskier nature of publishing a book versus publishing a journal. To put it bluntly (although there are exceptions), every work a publisher produces is a risk: spending money up front to produce a good (the book) that has no guarantee of sales recovering the costs to produce that book, much less make a profit. In fact, much academic monograph publishing doesn't cover its costs—nearly all university presses are subsidized by their parent university[2] and operate at a loss.

Think about it: journals publishers know (generally) what subscription revenue they will receive before they produce the content and understand whether it will prove to be sustainable. The journal is a brand—and it also has a built-in readership for every issue.

Therefore, every book is a risk, for unlike a journal, there is no existent subscription base. Unlike journal sales, we do not have a guaranteed, paid-in-advance market for our book content. Produce a journal article and you know that work has been paid for in advance. But in the book world, which actually has vastly more costs associated with producing content, there are simply no guarantees regarding sales levels. Publishers do their best to profile how we think a book will perform to decide whether we will invest in it, but nothing is sure. Approval plans were about the only predictable means of ensuring that some of the costs would be recovered. And those are continuing to decline rapidly.

The Costs of Producing a Monograph

In Feburary 2016, Ithaka S&R produced the most comprehensive report to date, examining the costs of producing high-quality monographs, using nearly 400 titles across 20 publishers as a base for research.[3] According to the study, publishing costs were the following:

Table 1. Full Cost of a High-Quality Digital Monograph (Excluding In-Kind Cost)

GROUP	GROUP AVERAGE	GROUP MEDIAN	95TH PERCENTILE	5TH PERCENTILE	HIGHEST COST TITLE	LOWEST COST TITLE
1	$30,091	$27,955	$57,991	$18,678	$65,921	$16,401
2	$44,906	$42,851	$69,417	$26,292	$129,909	$19,516
3	$34,098	$33,199	$53,084	$18,149	$76,537	$15,140
4	$49,155	$48,547	$73,885	$31,760	$99,144	$24,234

These costs are made up of expenses for copyediting, page composition, proofreading, and an author advance against royalties. The vast majority of the cost was staff time spent directly on monograph publishing, whether on acquisitions, manuscript editorial, design, production, or marketing activities.

The actual PPB (paper, printing, and binding) are almost insignificant, generally between $5.50 and $7.50 per printed book for a publisher the size of Oxford University Press (OUP), which has significant buying power. None of these costs are eliminated in the digital world. What library staff may also not recognize are the indirect costs associated with the publication of e-books. There is a cost associated with warehousing a digital object for eternity, and in fact, with the variety of different platforms, publishers actually have to produce multiple types of digital objects—XML, UPDF for institutional e-book aggregators, and epub3 for consumer e-book sellers. Publishers need to have the processes, people, and vendors to create all these formats. We have to have metadata warehousing and distribution—we are all now required to send our metadata to discoverability services, to the e-book aggregators, and to suppliers. In sales, we have to manage the relationships with the resellers and work closely with the library community to ensure that our business models, our content, and our services are what you need. Marketing also comes at a cost—our marketing team has to work closely with authors to ensure that those in the discipline are aware of the title. Marketing is far more important than ever before—if we are to be reliant on demand from users to drive any purchasing, we have to make sure they know a title is available and what it's about. Editorially, we work very closely with authors of every single book. At OUP, an additional layer of approval is needed for every single book: an author-written proposal must be approved by the delegates to the press (appointed senior scholars around the world who are tasked with the simple mission of ensuring OUP is producing publications of top quality). In addition, while royalties on sales of 500 copies sales may not make a significant difference in the life of an academic, royalties management does have to be executed. Publishers have a responsibility to the author to continue to manage that payment for as long as that work continues to sell, and there is a cost in doing that. When you produce a few thousand titles a year, or even a few hundred, that number rapidly multiplies. And all of these tasks are *not* disappearing in the digital era.

The costs of producing an electronic book do not magically disappear in this process, for an electronic book is merely the electronic version of an item that has already been produced in its printed form. Most academic works are still available in print format, so the fixed or up-front costs associated with publishing books in a print format are still incurred. At Oxford University Press, approximately 40 percent of all of our sales are still printed works, so the infrastructure dedicated to support the print format has not dwindled or subsided in recent years.

Monograph Sales—Predictability Lost

The sales profile of a typical academic monograph may surprise you: publishers will typically sell between 200 and 700 units of a monograph over a title's lifetime (yes, that's all). Between 75 and 80 percent of those sales occur in the first year. These are not considered profitable titles—not by any measure. To make it possible to produce books that are important but have a limited audience, university presses rely on the other types of works they publish: course-adopted titles or ones that end up getting a healthy "trade/consumer" profile. Publishers need these more mainstream books to support the otherwise very low-margin (if any) monographs. To a library purchaser, it's hard to tell the difference—libraries see these titles as works appropriate for an academic library. And typically, the other purchasers of these books are affiliated with a university (students or faculty).

In the past, publishers had the predictability of approval plans to help guide financial planning. We knew we would earn back a good portion of our investment in a reasonable amount of time. If we were publishing a philosophy book, we could predict that the approval-plan vendors would automatically purchase a certain number of copies. These year-one sales would then hopefully earn back the majority of our costs and our business wouldn't take a loss on the bottom line for money we'd invested that hadn't been returned (because anything you've invested that hasn't been earned back immediately with sales is a loss on your profitability and your bottom line.) Unearned royalties, where we haven't yet sold enough books to cover the advance on earnings paid to authors when a book is signed, are a significant negative on the balance sheet.

We all know that a monograph is not the heaviest-use item in libraries in the print world. They are, by design, specialized works appealing to a specialized audience, but to that audience, they are meaningful. Why such low use? Why do 30 to 40 percent of newly acquired monographs not circulate in libraries—according to data contained in reports distributed in library publications and conferences? One key factor could be that this content has been locked in their containers on the shelves of your libraries (the print book), and what's contained in those pages is discoverable by only a few mechanisms—the limited amount of metadata in your online catalogs (MARC [MAchine-Readable Cataloging] record, author, publication year, LC classes, and so on), the recommendation of faculty or librarians, book reviews, citations, reading lists, or a serendipitous discovery while browsing library shelves. How could potential readers ever have known, for example, that a philosophy book had important information about the Irish famine in one chapter? You couldn't—and it didn't get used, but that doesn't mean that it shouldn't have, for it was just tucked away where the reader couldn't be expected to find it. It can sometimes take years for academic monographs to get reviewed in the important publications in their disciplines—another important factor when thinking about the life cycle of monograph content.

Usage-Based Acquisition of Monographs

Publishers now need to plan for use-based purchasing models, particularly for content that was considered low use in the library (monographs) as opposed to the high-use items (journals). Why is this such a problem for publishers? Look back to the economic model—publishers try to recoup their costs quickly because it is so expensive to produce a book and no guarantee of a return on that investment. If too many books don't support themselves, it means serious financial trouble for that publisher. Moreover, if a publisher doesn't experience ample sales in a reasonable amount of time (preferably in the first year), it will unequivocally impact everything else a publisher does. On the library side, the fundamental theory of "don't pay until it gets used" resonated with libraries that had been struggling with their circulation statistics not bearing out the tremendous investment they had made in books in the past. Publishers, meanwhile, have to understand that as libraries deal with reduced budgets, budgets have been further challenged by an increasing percentage spent on journals. There is no easy answer to this dilemma.

In the old world (pre-demand-driven purchasing), the publisher's profile of a title's sales for a profit and loss statement would look like Table 2. This table shows that most sales are realized during year one, hopefully earning back the majority of the up-front costs, and the publisher doesn't take a loss on the bottom line for money that's been invested but hasn't been returned in the form of a sale of the book. Table 3 shows what happens in the DDA world, where there is zero predictability and no sense of how long it's going to take publishers to recoup their costs. While there is an understanding of why the model appeals to librarians, this should serve as an illustration of why it does introduce risk beyond anything we've seen before for publishers. It doesn't mean that publishers shouldn't experiment (and many have and continue to do so) with demand-driven models but illuminates that there are valid concerns about the long-term viability of this model.

Table 2. Approval Plan World

3 YEAR SALES	YEAR 1	YEAR 2	YEAR 3	TOTAL
Domestic	400	75	25	500
Export	75			75
Total	475	75	25	575

Table 3. Demand-Driven Purchasing World

3 YEAR SALES	YEAR 1	YEAR 2	YEAR 3	TOTAL
Domestic	?	?	?	??
Export	?	?	?	??
Total	??	??	??	??

To succinctly summarize, with the old business model there was a high degree of predictability in fixed costs and sales, and now the only predictable thing for publishers are costs.

Risks from e-book models aside, there is tremendous opportunity for this type of content in the digital environment. I am bullish about the opportunities digital content presents to actually help long-form scholarship survive and indeed thrive; we can far better expose users to what's in the pages of books they never would have found before. That's actually the primary reason OUP invested in the XML platform for University Press Scholarship Online and why we have taken that investment and shared it with the wider university press community (in University Press Scholarship Online), taking our role as the largest university press seriously and understanding that smaller university presses don't have the resources to do this on their own. A key component is having authors write abstracts for every single chapter and creating keywords for each chapter that are connected across the whole database so users can see what these authors feel are the core ideas of their writing, not generated by a computer, and so incredibly valuable to long-form scholarship. For users, the key issue may not be getting the book they want electronically but finding the book they wanted in the first place.

We need to be realistic about what is possible and we need to keep our minds open. What we don't want is to simply carry on with print models in digital form as if they are one and the same. We have just begun to scratch the surface of what is possible in a digital environment for all forms of scholarly communication, and certainly new models and new modes of accessibility will arise that have not even been thought of yet.

The Future

» Publishers will take a more conservative approach to demand-driven models moving forward; the current DDA model is not financially sustainable for most, if not all, academic publishers.

» I firmly believe that we will continue to see new models in book selling come and go and that this iterative cycle of acceptance, rejection, and modification is something we will all need to learn to live with.

» Unfortunately, the reduction of spending on books will force publishers to take fewer chances publishing esoteric academic works that do not have a predictable market.

Notes

1. Oxford Dictionaries Online, http://www.oxforddictionaries.com/us/definition/american_english/monograph (Accessed May 2016).

2. Sherman, Scott. "University Presses Under Fire." *The Nation* (May 6, 2014). https://www.thenation.com/article/university-presses-under-fire (Accessed May 2016).

3. Maron, Nancy L., Christine Mulhern, Daniel Rossman, and Kimberly Schmelzinger. "The Costs of Publishing Monographs: Toward a Transparent Methodology." *Ithaka S+R*. Last Modified February 5, 2016. http://dx.doi.org/10.18665/sr.276785 (Accessed May 2016).

13

MORE THAN LIBRARIES: COPYRIGHT, LICENSING, AND THE KEY TO ANCILLARY REVENUE

Carol S. Richman

///////////// TOP TAKEAWAYS IN THIS CHAPTER

» What it's like to work in the field of licensing if you work for a publisher

» Licensing also includes types of agreements between libraries and publishers

» Many forms of licensing will earn revenue for published works

» Understand the basics of copyright and why it's important

The field of publishing has many intricate pieces, some of which go unnoticed by most librarians. Like a pie chart, the pieces fit together to form a published work for which many revenue opportunities exist. What exactly are those opportunities and how does this fit into a publishing plan? In this chapter we will explore those far-reaching opportunities and what it means for a published work, whether a book, journal, journal articles, or a work in another medium. There are numerous ways publishers make money besides selling directly to libraries. For example, there are generally three or four different areas of responsibility in a rights department, the department most often tasked with monetizing works besides the traditional "sales" department: licensing, permissions, sales support, and translations. Each area has its own focus and general goals and objectives. Each also has an array of challenges and opportunities. Additionally, there may be some overlap within each of the areas.

How to Make Money: Licensing

Once publishers have a work assigned to them via copyright transfer or an exclusive right to publish agreement, the work goes through an intensive production cycle. This includes peer review, typesetting, printing, indexing, electronic hosting, publication, and archiving. Once the work is published and is ready for prime time, it also opens the door to explore other avenues for selling and distributing a work.

Let's imagine that we are a publisher and have produced works to disseminate to our customers. We can sell directly to customers, but we can also research and take advantage of other avenues available to the publishing industry. When thinking about the different types of opportunities to sell or license content, it's important to remember to build key relationships with those individuals with whom you will be negotiating. This is key to the success of any licensing programs. What follows are different types of opportunities.

Direct Selling

Direct selling enables a publisher's sales force to sell to a known customer base such as academic libraries. This approach may be the most familiar to librarians. With a sales force in place, deals can be made directly with libraries so that their user communities can access the content the publisher is selling. Typically, these types of deals are finalized by negotiating sales agreements and the length of the term of the agreement differs from customer to customer; common terms are three to five years for journal packages, although some prefer new agreements each year. Sales agreements (or license agreements) are legal documents signed by each party to set terms for pricing, use, delivery, and content. These types of deals are extremely common for online books, journals, and video products. The types of licenses used can be straightforward and easily finalized, or, on the other end of the spectrum, they can be complicated and take quite a lot of time to execute. As in any negotiation process, the completion of such agreements depends upon each party's expectations and their respective demands. What stands out as a premium need in an agreement between a library and a publisher are two items: the fee and the terms of use.

When negotiating fees, generally speaking, many factors are at play. Fees are not only important to a publisher but also to the librarian negotiating the purchase. For instance, a particular institution and library may have a long-standing relationship. In the world of journals, a library may be interested in the entire list of journals or discipline-specific titles, or an ad-hoc. This holds true for books as well.

There may also be other factors: whether the library is a college (a four-year institution) or a university with graduate schools (i.e., advanced degrees, law school, or degrees in medicine). Additionally, one might consider the size of the population at an institution.

Fees for journal subscriptions are typically negotiated. The fees may be based on content usage, which, in turn, is based on a current usage report of subscribed journals, or they may be based on a total list of journals (typically called the Big Deal). Fees for the purchase of books or videos are negotiated and are usually purchased based on specific disciplines.

Terms of Use or Authorized Use of Licensed Materials are also negotiated; these include a list of how a publisher and the library expect the content to be used. Following are some of the items that a librarian may feel important to include in an agreement, as they outline how content can and should be used by the library's community:

» Analysis. Authorized Users [those members of the institution and the library's community] shall be permitted to extract or use information contained in the Licensed Materials for educational, scientific, or research purposes, including but not limited to extraction and manipulation of information for the purposes of illustration, explanation, example, comment, criticism, teaching, research, or analysis.

» *Course Packs.* Licensee, the Institutions, and Authorized Users may use a Reasonable Amount of the Licensed Materials in the preparation of Course Packs or other educational materials. [In order to use the complete body of a work, a separate permission would be needed.]

» Digitally Copy. Licensee, the Institutions, and Authorized Users may download and digitally copy a Reasonable Amount of the Licensed Materials.

» Display. Licensee, the Institutions, and Authorized Users shall have the right to electronically display the Licensed Materials.

» Electronic Reserve. Licensee, the Institutions, and Authorized Users may use a Reasonable Amount of the Licensed Materials in connection with specific courses of instruction offered by Licensee.

» Inter-Library Loan (ILL). The Institutions shall be permitted to use Reasonable Amounts of the Licensed Materials to fulfill occasional requests from other, nonparticipating institutions, a practice commonly called Inter-Library Loan. Customer agrees to fulfill such requests in compliance with Section 108 of the United States Copyright Law (17 USC §108, "Limitations on exclusive rights: Reproduction by libraries and archives") and the Guidelines for the Proviso of Subsection 108(2g)(2) prepared by the National Commission on New Technological Uses of Copyrighted Works (CONTU).

» Print Copy. Licensee, the Institutions and Authorized Users may print a Reasonable Amount of the Licensed Materials.

» Recover Copying Costs. Licensee and the Institutions may charge a reasonable fee to cover costs of copying or printing portions of Licensed Materials for Authorized Users.

» Scholarly Sharing. Authorized Users may transmit to a third-party colleague in hard copy or electronically, minimal, insubstantial amounts of the Licensed Materials for personal use or scholarly, educational, or scientific research or professional use but in no case for resale or commercial purposes. In addition, Authorized Users have the right to use, with appropriate credit, figures, tables, and brief excerpts from the Licensed Materials in the Authorized User's own scientific, scholarly and educational works.

» Text and Data Mining. Authorized Users may use the licensed material to perform and engage in text mining/data mining activities for legitimate academic research and other educational purposes.

Agreements for the purchase of content may be called a *license agreement* or a *sales agreement*. The elements of a license or sales agreement are similar. What's of primary importance in negotiating such agreements is the point that each party become familiar with the other so that there is an understanding of expectations and a successful negotiation. It is helpful to work directly with sales staff and involve them when negotiating an agreement with a librarian. In order to close a deal and have a smooth transition, publishers should work directly with library staff and get to know them—it will greatly help. It will also help to get to know the key players in a library consortium.

Now, consider how many global libraries and consortia exist and then imagine trying to reach all of them. Will your direct selling approach and marketing department be able to reach everyone on a global level or are there other ways to get the content to readers or potential customers?

Subsidiary Rights Licensing

Subsidiary rights licensing is the act of licensing books, journals, or videos to another party in order to increase revenue and disseminate content through multiple channels. The revenue generated by these activities is typically called ancillary or incremental income, and while it can add up to a lot of revenue and help maximize sales, it probably should not be considered the primary source of publishing income.

Licensing to content aggregators or third-party vendors has gained much acceptance over the years. A third-party vendor can take much of the burden of direct selling off a publisher's plate. These types of vendors may be interested in discipline-specific content or all of your published content. Learning about what a vendor does, their sales force, how they reach the market, and their financial offers is an important factor to the success of this type of license deal.

Before entering into such a deal, which typically lasts three to five years, it would also be important to determine how potential customers (academic or corporate libraries) might feel about purchasing from a vendor who represents many publishers instead of buying directly from a publisher. Making contact with vendor decision makers is highly important as it typically takes a long time to negotiate these deals. As someone who might be in charge of negotiating such a deal, you'd be expected to secure internal buy-in among your peers and management, especially the sales team and those responsible for the content. Of course, licensing content to aggregators does not preclude direct buying and selling.

In addition, third-party vendors usually negotiate sales agreements with their customers. Like the terms of use mentioned earlier, a vendor usually has in place an end user license agreement (EULA) that specifies the allowed uses for the content. When negotiating a license agreement with a vendor, it is important to review their EULA to make sure that it favorably compares to one that you use in your agreements. What economic thinking goes into choosing to sell direct versus licensing through a third party?

Foreign Translations Rights

Yet another revenue opportunity for monetizing licensing activities is selling translations rights, which allow foreign publishers to translate, sell, and distribute the content. Most scholarly communication is published in English; however, for various reasons many users and third-party aggregators are interested in translating these works into other languages. How does a publisher go about doing this? Networking at industry meetings will help a publisher meet individuals representing companies who do this type of work. There are worldwide meetings to help one accomplish this, such as the London and Frankfurt Book Fairs and BEA (Book Expo America). These meetings are well established and are great places to make connections.

Are translations rights worth the effort? Absolutely! Revenue earned from these deals falls to the bottom line. You can sign a lot of translation deals for a popular book. Any translation deal can be lucrative as the internal cost to conduct this type of business is low. Before offering a title to a foreign publisher for translation, make sure that products you might promote have been cleared for translations rights. It is important to check the actual publishing agreement, as some authors may retain translations rights and others may not allow a work to be translated. Additionally, there are authors who want to approve all translations deals. All of these points should be covered in the author/publisher agreement. This is extremely important as librarians worldwide will only buy authorized translated works that have no rights issues.

When promoting and selling translations, it is important to do a bit of research into prospective companies with which to partner and to keep in mind some general guidelines regarding licensing translations. The most important thing to know is that you cannot license the translation rights for the same title in one language to more than one publisher. So, if you license the French language rights to a French publisher, you cannot license that title to another French publisher until the first publisher's agreement ends or is terminated.

Here are some suggestions when considering promoting works to a foreign publisher for translation who will then sell the translated work in their market:

» Make sure that the publisher can sell the rights to allow foreign publishers to translate, publish, sell, and distribute content. Foreign publishers will want world rights to the title in their language. They will not want to sell it just in their country but throughout the world.

» Payments for this right include an upfront payment, called an advance, as well as future royalties that will be paid after the book has sold and the advance has earned out. Advances are based on the print run and the retail price at which a foreign publisher will be selling their edition. Royalties are usually between 7 and 10 percent and are negotiable. Royalties will not usually start coming in until at least a year after publication.

» Print runs will vary by publisher, and generally an advance is expected for quantities of 500 copies or more. If a publisher is only going to print a small number, then a flat fee is usually paid with no future royalties.

» Media rights:
   ◆ Selling audiobooks is a multimillion-dollar industry—and it continues to grow.
   ◆ Many large-print publishers also have audio imprints.
   ◆ Like print contracts, audio contracts have clauses for advances and royalties.

» Research what types of content a publisher has translated in the past and become familiar with their overall publishing program.

» Identify key decision makers and make appointments with them (in person at trade shows, via phone, or contact them by e-mail) in order to discuss business partnerships and options.

» Produce an annual catalog outlining new titles available for translations. This can be sent out as a PDF document and does not have to be a formally printed catalog; this will help keep your costs down. You can always print it out yourself as needed, but sending a PDF file has become standard practice.

» Meet with key internal stakeholders, such as editors and marketing staff, and keep everyone informed.

» Meet with authors to discuss the potential for selling translation rights. Authors are a great wealth of information and may have insight into foreign companies interested in translating specific works.

When you send a work out to a company for translation as an option, remember to put a time limit on the decision to translate, as other companies might be interested in the same title. A typical decision time frame is three months but could be as long as six months. Remember to track all activity on translation options. If a potential publisher turns you down on a title, you will be prepared to send the title to another potential translation partner. A good rule of thumb is to first approach those with whom you have an established track record to determine interest. Following through on these types of deals is important. Your colleagues, and the author, will want to be informed of any project progress.

Copyrights

Why is holding a copyright important? A copyright is important as it means that a publisher has secured the right to publish and distribute works, and librarians who purchase content are able to trust that the work is legally protected. Who should care about copyrights? The simple answer to this is that everyone should care. While publishers go to great efforts to publish, market, sell, and license works, it is important that librarians or buyers of content can be confident that the content is protected by law.

According to the U.S. Constitution (1), the Copyright Law and Act (2) exists in order to protect original works that are fixed in a tangible medium (written down on paper or in a digital document). Copyright is an author or owner's legal right to reproduce, display, transmit, prepare derivative works, or modify a work the owner has created. Without copyright protection, publishers cannot expect to publish a work and make money on that publication.

The basic concept of copyright is that copyright equals protected ownership. Ownership of a work generally remains with an author unless the rights have been transferred by means of an agreed contract to another party, such as a publisher, or unless the work is made as a "work made for hire," as in the example of a work created while employed by another party. However, an author may choose to retain the copyright of his or her work but assign the exclusive right to publish and disseminate the work to a publisher.

Below are a few key terms and regulations that can help you understand the basics of copyright:

Copyright Terms:
» Copyright: Owner's legal right to reproduce, display, transmit, perform, and modify a work.

» Fair Use: The section of copyright law that enables you to make legal use of copyrighted materials without payment or permission; an example of this is for educational purposes.

» Exemption: A legal term for an exemption to the general rule—for example, Fair Use.

» Public Domain: A term that classifies works no longer under copyright protection (e.g., an expired copyright) or a work that was published by the U.S. federal government.

Section 102(a) of the Copyright Act states that the following works are protected by copyright law:

» Literary works (including compilations and computer programs)
» Musical works (including accompanying words)
» Dramatic works (including accompanying music)
» Pantomime and choreographic works
» Pictorial, graphic, and sculptural works
» Motion picture and other audiovisual works
» Sound recordings
» Architectural works

Section 102(b) of the Copyright Act states the following are not protected:

» Works not fixed in a tangible form of expression

» Titles, names, short phrases, slogans, or familiar symbols or designs (these items may be protected under trademark or service mark laws)

» Listings of ingredients or contents (these may be protected under trade secret law)

» Ideas, procedures, methods, systems, processes, concepts, principles, discoveries, or devices (these items may be protected under patent law)

» Standard calendars, rulers, lists, or tables taken from public domain documents or sources and other works containing no original authorship

In the United States, all works are registered with the U.S. Copyright Office at the Library of Congress. Either an author or a publisher may register a work. This provides registered protection for content—you cannot go to court and sue for infringement damages without your work having been registered. As an extra level of insurance, all published and salable/downloadable content (whether print or electronic) should always have an identifier, such as an International Standard Book Number (ISBN) or International Standard Serial Number (ISSN). Any unauthorized use of a copyrighted work that violates the copyright owner's exclusive rights in the work constitutes infringement.

Examples of infringement include unauthorized copies of an original work for commercial purposes, adapting someone else's original work, and outright plagiarism. Infringing on someone else's work is a serious offense and may result in consequences such as legal action, financial damages or restoration request, loss of reputation, career limitations, or all of these.

Fair use doctrine means you can use a work without permission in these circumstances: criticism or reviews of or comments about the work, news reporting (reporting about the work), for teaching purposes, or part of scholarship or research. Claiming fair use is dependent on the purpose and character of the use, including whether it is for commercial, nonprofit, or educational purposes; the nature of the original copyrighted work; the amount and substantiality of the portion used in relation to the copyrighted work as a whole; and the effect of the use on the potential market for, or value of, the copyrighted work.

Permissions

If one cannot claim that the use of a work or portion of a work is fair use, then the writer must ask for permission to reuse part of a work. What needs written permission? Adaptations of original source material using someone else's expression of ideas and words require permission, as does the reproduction and use of charts, graphs, images, and so on, for purposes of for-profit outcome, and the repeated (more than one time) reproduction of models, process diagrams, and so on, in educational material or content otherwise defined as fair use.

If you are unsure, what you want to use probably needs permission, so use common sense. Written permission must be received before the portion being used is to be published. Proper attribution must be given in the new published work per the following:

>> Title of original source
>> Author of original source
>> Publisher of original source
>> Publication date of original source
>> Page number of original source
>> The phrase "used or adapted with permission"

What doesn't require permission and attribution? You do not have to cite sources for facts that are readily available from numerous sources or that are considered common knowledge. There are many facts available by doing searches on the Internet; these would include facts found in newspapers or reported by news sources that have been commonly publicized.

When you need to get permission, you need to know the following:

>> Who owns the authority for permission? This information can be found at the front of a journal or book (within the front matter).
>> Who can grant or confirm authority for the permission (often different than the copyright owner)? If the work has been published, the publisher usually grants permission.
>> Can you obtain permission in writing? You should obtain permission in writing, but receiving permission via an e-mail is also acceptable.

It is important to keep in mind some copyright reminders. Works do not need a formal copyright mark to be covered by copyright laws. Cite the source and use quotation marks whenever you "borrow" information from someone else's work. Just because it is online and available for free does not mean it is available for distribution or reuse. Obtain permission to use other's people's intellectual property. The penalties for breaking copyright laws are severe. With copyright protection in place, an author or owner can explore various types of opportunities that can result in increasing readership to a wide range of audiences and will increase revenue.

The Future

» While copyright may be at the center of which content is disseminated, I believe there will be a shift and many more authors will insist on retaining copyright

» I think it will become easier to license or buy works. I have always held a theory about content ownership and the ability to purchase content. So, let us imagine an enormous three-dimensional bicycle wheel with lots of spokes and sections. Each of those spokes and sections might represent content. The center of the spoke might represent the content distributors (e.g., authors, publishers, libraries, aggregators, and third-party vendors). Users could search the global world of publications and easily link to content. Do I think copyright will still exist? Yes, of course.

» But, I think in the future content users will find easier solutions to find what they need and be able to purchase or license content

Further Readings

Association of American Publishers. www.publishers.org (Accessed July 2016).

Association of Learned and Society Publishers. www. alpsp.org (Accessed July 2016).

Authors Guild. www. authorsguild.org (Accessed July 2016).

Copyright Clearance Center. www. copyright.com (Accessed July 2016).

Copyright Law of the United States of America, Title 17 of the *United States Code.* http://copyright.gov/title17/92preface.html (Accessed July 2016).

Creative Commons. www. creativecommons.org (Accessed July 2016).

CrossRef. www. crossref.org (Accessed July 2016).

International Association of Scientific, Technical, and Medical Publishers. www.stm-assoc.org (Accessed July 2016).

Publishers Licensing Society. www.pls.org.uk (Accessed July 2016).

SHERPA (promotes open access). www.sherpa.ac.uk (Accessed July 2016).

Society for Scholarly Publishing (SSP). www. sspnet.org (Accessed July 2016).

U.S. Constitution, Article I, Section 8.

U.S. Copyright Office. www.copyright.gov (Accessed July 2016).

14

SALES: THE ROAD OFT TRAVELED

Jenni Wilson

sales·per·son \-ˌpər-sᵊn\ An individual who sells goods and services to other entities. The successfulness of a salesperson is usually measured by the amount of sales he or she is able to make during a given period and how good that person is in persuading individuals to make a purchase. If a salesperson is employed by a company, in some cases compensation can be decreased or increased based on the amount of goods or services sold.

—BusinessDictionary.com

But I am a librarian. I tell people that proudly, but also with a tiny bit of guilt. I have guilt because though I do have my library degree, I haven't worked in libraries since my earliest days as an assistant librarian in a two-person corporate library in Houston, Texas. I like to identify myself as a librarian because librarians are some of the smartest, most thoughtful, and funniest people I know and I want to be considered part of that crowd. And, well, I do have a library degree. But instead of working in a library in a traditional librarian role, I sell stuff to libraries. It has allowed me to roam freely in the Land-of-Libraries and to learn more than I might have ever known if I had settled in as a cataloger, which is what I thought I wanted to do. Luckily for me, I like being on the road and meeting new and different people all the time. I like standing in front of a group of people and presenting my product. I like attending conferences and wandering the aisles of the vendor exhibits during my downtime, finding out what is new and what our competitors are doing (and picking up free books). So I definitely found a career that is right for me.

How I Got Here

So how does a person find their path to becoming a library partner representative, consulting with them and selling products and services, when all they ever really wanted to do was be a librarian? I have to imagine that there are thousands of reasons that are as varied as those that apply to finding any job. My journey began on an airplane. I had been out of college a couple of years and was stuck on a plane on the tarmac at O'Hare, trying to get to Minneapolis during a snowstorm. Those were the days when it was still legal to hold passengers on a delayed plane for five or six hours without allowing anyone to escape to the terminal. So, as one is wont to do in these situations (or at least I am, and I realize that I am often despised for this), I started talking to the guy sitting next to me. He was a librarian, and I fell in love. Not with him, mind you, but with the idea of being a librarian. Why it had not occurred to me before that this was a good career option for me was a little strange, given that I had worked in my college library for all four years of my tenure there, including in one shady excuse-for-a-library during a year abroad in Italy. Maybe the mind-numbing job of updating loose-leaf service binders with breaking tax law content turned me off to the idea for a few years, but I made the decision then and there, on that plane, that this was what I was going to do.

So I left my very glamorous career in transportation sales, selling space on container ships to liquor importers and distributors, to pursue a higher calling—to be a librarian! When I told my boss at the shipping company that I was leaving my job to go to library school, he looked at me kind of funny and asked if I was really going to prison or something. To him, they were one and the same.

After I received my Master of Science in Library and Information Science (MS/LIS) from the University of Illinois, I headed down to Houston, Texas, where I got a job in the petroleum and engineering library at a big oil company, which I loved. I got to have my hands in a little bit of everything, including cataloging and reference and "Selective Dissemination of Information," for example, photocopying the tables of contents from newly arrived journals and sending them around the company via inter-office mail. The engineers would highlight the articles that were of interest to them and I would make sure that the journal was ready and waiting for them when they came to the library to pick it up. But, no offense Texans, Houston just wasn't my cup of tea, so I headed back to Chicago, where I assumed that quickly finding a corporate librarian job was a reasonable expectation. Little did I know. When I did hit the job market, I found myself in a real jam. I was looking for a position in a corporate library but found myself in a kind of catch-22 situation, where I didn't have enough experience working in libraries for anyone to want to hire me (even though I had "mad" Dialog skills and could build a mean search) but I couldn't get any more experience if no one would hire me. I tried stressing my previous work experience in corporate sales in the shipping industry but that got me nowhere, and I worked for a librarian temp agency doing a few stints in local public library branches, but that wasn't paying the bills.

Then I came across a position on the American Library Association (ALA) Job Line. In the old days, you had to call a phone number, listen to a person read out a really long listing of jobs, and write down all the details of ones that might be of interest. I listened to one description from a New York–based subscription agency that I had never even heard of that was looking for a Midwest sales representative who had both an MLS degree—check—and sales experience—check. And while it was never my intention to re-enter the world of sales (which, by the way, my mother claims is a career I was destined for, because when I was 7 or 8 years old, I managed to sell 80 gazillion boxes of Girl Scout cookies before I got kicked out of the troop . . . but that's another story). I thought, well, I can take this job, and then at least I'll get to hang out with librarians until I can find my way back in as a librarian somewhere. So much for that plan.

What I Do

When I was asked to write this chapter, it was with the idea that I would be talking to both new and veteran librarians, helping them make sense of the brochure-toting, smooth talkers who are seemingly constantly harassing you for meetings. And while I obviously can't speak for everyone, I can speak as someone who has been on the road selling to libraries for nearly 25 years. People have all kinds of ideas about the type of person who chooses a career in sales, just like people have ideas about why people become lawyers or why they become librarians. No one goes into sales because they want to be the guy who, when the person they're calling realizes who it is, makes them regret having picked up the phone. And I can say with confidence that it is rarely a salesperson's intention to try to put one over on you, or to sell you something that your library really doesn't need just so they can make money. In my and most of my colleagues' cases, it is with a healthy dose of humility and respect for your time that we hope to introduce you to a product or service that will fill the specific needs of your library and the university community at large. And while it may seem to be that, in some cases, our organizations' goals are at odds with one another—corporate profits versus educating the masses—the two of us need each other, and developing a mutually respectful relationship with sales representatives can be both satisfying and lucrative for all parties.

For many people, the life of a salesperson might seem pretty exciting, maybe even glamourous. We fly around the country, visiting libraries and attending big conferences. We swan into the library bearing gifts of swag and invitations to lunch. We're often entertaining at the ALA show, hosting lovely dinners and dessert receptions. And while that must look like fun from the outside (and, frankly, it really can be a lot of fun), a lot of preparation goes into these meetings and events. While we show up in your office with smiles on our faces and enthusiasm to spare, it is often after having driven around campus for 45 minutes, desperately looking for parking, then sprinting to the library in heels, mopping the sweat off of our faces before meeting you. And trying to find the best restaurants in the conference city for breakfasts, lunches, and dinners, securing reservations at the right times, and juggling invitations and RSVPs for two or three or four venues can by trying. We want everyone to have a good time and we fret over who should sit where. It can be like planning a wedding but for multiple nights in a row. It's exhausting.

Of course, the life of the librarian is often misunderstood, too. The fact that when you tell someone you're a librarian and they say, "Oh, you must really love to read," has to be maddening. Is that what you think a librarian does all day? Read? I have seen the transition from the card catalog to the Online Public Access Catalog (OPAC). I have seen the migration from CD-ROM towers to full-text electronic databases. I have seen hard copies of the *Statistical Abstracts of the United States* weeded from the shelf but resurrected in electronic form. Journals and books have been moved into storage to make way for learning community spaces and coffee shops (which I love, thank you very much) and instead you have "big deal" electronic journal collections. Many serials librarians have become electronic resources librarians. Libraries are now engaged in marketing their services, proving their ROI (return on investment), and employing user experience experts. The things that are being sold to you are no longer simple—it's not just a book, it's an approval plan, it's DDA, it's short-term loans, just-in-time, or just-in-case. In other words, it is not your granddaddy's library, that's for sure. As salespersons we have to keep pace with these changes and accompany you along the way. If we're lucky enough, we come to you presenting a product that we love because of its amazing content or because it's a terrific service that is beneficial to the librarian and the end users.

But before all the fun—and the work—can start, there has to be a plan. So how do we decide whom to approach to ask for meetings and when? That depends on a lot of variables. Those of us with small territories, just one state or two, are able to see our customers on a more regular basis and can use our thorough knowledge of your library's wants and needs and our understanding of your buying cycles to determine what to present and when. And we're able to get to know each of you on a more personal basis.

For those of us with bigger territories—I've covered as many as 19 states in one job—it is a bit more complicated to set our schedules. Usually you take a look at your entire territory and make a very rough outline of when you'd like to visit each state over the next year. Then you start looking at quarters, seeing what your goals are, and strategically deciding which regions to cover first. Once you get to individual months, you need to decide which parts of the states that you've mapped to those months you'll visit first. And then which customers. Normally we will target one or two bigger accounts in an area, try to set a meeting there first, and then build the rest of the trip around that. So while it might seem like your sales rep is being obnoxious, contacting you two or three times about setting up a meeting before you've had a chance to look at your calendar, mostly they're just trying to plan their travel and they want to do it in as geographically sensible a way as possible. And you might be the first piece of that puzzle.

If our biggest customer says no to a meeting, then we have to reconsider visiting that state until the chips fall into place, which means going back to your rough calendar and reconfiguring. Once we do get those first couple of pieces in place, though, it gets easier. Of course, it is always best to leave plenty of time between one meeting and the next (easier said than done) so that you don't have to sprint away from one library and drive at break-neck speed to the next. So we ask for your forgiveness if we ever seem anxious to wrap up a meeting, or if we arrive red-faced and panting.

So, now, whom do we see? Depending on the product or service that we're selling, we might want to meet with the person who heads up collection development, or maybe individual subject selectors/liaisons. It might make more sense, though, to meet with the head of acquisitions or electronic resources. In a smaller library we may be seeing the director. Since all libraries have their own structure and unique processing flows, it's not always easy to know whom to approach first. I know that I certainly appreciate when the head of collection development steers me to acquisitions or e-resources or a selector, etc., and vice versa.

So, as you can see, this process of meeting planning can be very time-consuming and complicated. While we can't always do everything in a completely orderly manner, we do try to minimize our company's expenses by being efficient. At the end of the day, we aim to be as productive as possible in the shortest time possible so that you can get back to your job and we can move on to our next meeting.

But after all of that planning and setting up meetings, what makes me a "good" salesperson? On a very basic level, it helps to be friendly, articulate, and approachable. But once we get in the door you'll find that a good salesperson will let you talk as much as or more than we do. If a salesperson is paying attention to you and is actually hearing what you say, then you know you've got a good one. Our job is not just to sell you stuff, rather it is to help you work out problems. The more we know about your library and your particular situation, the more we're able to offer ideas based on experiences that we've had with other customers. We're willing to dig in on our end to make things work for you. There must be nothing more frustrating than agreeing to meet with a salesperson and then finding that they are not prepared. We might not know much or anything about your library, or even not know enough about our own products. A good salesperson should always do their homework to understand what might be causing you pain and/or what might enhance your offerings to end users. We should be prepared to answer questions, but if we can't answer a question, we need to find the answer and get back to you with it quickly.

Some companies are large enough that the salesperson has one job—to visit customers and to present products/services, and that's it—and there are a whole slew of people on the back end who are dealing with technical issues, with billing, with renewals, and with proposal pricing. But even though those things are "not their job," a good salesperson will always know what is happening with your account before the sales call begins and after it is over. We might not be doing any of the background work (which is important to note, because most salespeople really can't fix your access issues—we have to rely on our sometimes completely swamped colleagues to do that work) but we should know who is doing the work and when to intervene and escalate if necessary. No one likes the boy who cries wolf all the time, so a good salesperson knows how to use those powers judiciously.

How You Can Help

On the other hand, what makes a "good" customer? A good customer is someone who is straightforward and honest but not abusive (you'd be surprised). If the library really doesn't have any use for a salesperson's product, then they should let us know so as to avoid wasting time and raising hopes. But a good customer is also open to new ideas and is willing to listen and learn because our products could be a great fit for the institution. If it is simply not the right time for a library to engage our services, but there is genuine interest, it is always appreciated when librarians are honest about that and are open to continuing the discussion at a later time. It allows us to keep you informed of product enhancements or service changes that might influence your decision one way or the other. Honesty and openness always win the day. You probably know that all salespeople are given goals at the beginning of each year, both in units and dollars, and that we have a sales pipeline that feeds those goals.

It is important for us to know that a potential sale is not completely dead so that we can show our managers that we do have prospects, and therefore they should continue to employ us because we are working hard!

Another trait of a good customer is to have as much respect for a sales-person's profession as we do for yours. Having driven through the Ozark Mountains in the snow, seeing flashing neon signs all along the way telling me how many people had died so far that year on that very road, only to show up at the library to be told that the person with whom I had an appointment was too busy to meet with me, well, that made me sad. It seems to show a real misunderstanding of the time and effort that goes into planning and preparing for sales calls and it suggests that what we do for a living is not thought of as important. This is just one tale of woe, but things like that happen more often than you might think. Obviously it is understood that stuff happens, people get ill, or the dean of the library or the president of the university needs you in a meeting. But simply making a phone call or sending an e-mail calling off a meeting is all that is needed to ensure that no one is left standing at the front desk feeling both disappointed and frustrated. We're not a bunch of crybabies, but we are human, and we do take pride in our work and get hurt feelings. No cupcakes for you!

Speaking of cupcakes, a lot of the fun of a sales job is getting to know our customers, allowing you to know us, and building a relationship of trust. We sometimes come bearing treats not only because we want you to like us but because we understand that sometimes it is just nice to have someone give you a cookie. Having lunches and dinners together, especially outside the library at conferences, is also fun because you can relax and get to know one another as people and not just as customers/salespeople. When you find out that you have hobbies in common, or that you went to the same college, or that you both have cats named Ralph, it just makes your work seem less trans-actional and more like consulting with a person who you know and like. When you trust each other, for real, it makes doing business less stressful. And doing business does not have to be nor should it be stressful. Ultimately, we both have our own agendas, ours to sell our products/services, and yours to get a good deal for your library on that much-needed product/service. And while we shouldn't spend a lot of time being frivolous and wasteful, it is nice to have fun along the way if you can. I like to laugh, I like to eat, I like to enjoy the occasional cocktail, and I'm guessing that many of you do, too.

But while it is nice to rack up frequent flyer miles and hotel points (if you're lucky enough to work for a company that lets you keep your miles) and to eat yummy meals (when you're not eating at Taco Bell), all of that travel can make you more than a little bit loopy from time to time. It is easy to mix up time zones or to go to the wrong hotel (regular Marriott versus Courtyard by Marriott). Sometimes you even end up in the wrong city! I have left phones and lumbar pillows and jackets on planes. I have left articles of clothing and shoes in hotels. I have had my luggage lost, and even destroyed, on more than one occasion. And sometimes I have just done stupid things, like the time that I was seated on a plane and a woman was in the aisle making her way to her seat when she had to stop next to me. She looked so familiar so I gave her a smile and said, "I know you but I can't remember where we've met. Are you a librarian?" She looked at me and said, "No, I'm the United States senator from Missouri." Oh. You're Claire McCaskill. Oops. Carry on, Senator. Days like that make you oh so grateful to the flight attendant who offers you a free drink on your flight home because they can tell that you've really had a day.

So I'd say to you who are wondering why we do what we do, the answer is—for a bunch of different reasons. For those of us with both a library degree and sales experience, some have hunkered down in sales and others have moved back and forth between the two worlds. And while I envy the latter, I find myself in the former positon, having not turned back once since I landed in my first library sales job. There is an unfortunate tendency in our business to refer to those of us who work with publishers, booksellers, and integrated library system (ILS) producers as being from the "Dark Side," and I really don't like that. It's not at all dark over here. We are generally a bunch of sunshine-loving folks who have a real interest in libraries, whether because we are librarians ourselves or because we're interested in publishing or enterprise software. I try to immerse myself in library-related activities as much as my job will allow, by belonging to interest groups and serving on their boards. Organizations like the ALA, Special Libraries Association (SLA), American Association of Law Libraries (AALL), NASIG (formerly the North American Serials Interest Group, Inc.), UKSG (United Kingdom Serials Group), and more are delighted to have those of us from the vendor community participate in whatever way we can, bringing our unique perspective to their communities. I've also had the pleasure of speaking to classes at library schools, explaining to them what it is that I do and why I play an intricate role in the life cycle of the library.

At the end of the day, I can't say that this is the life that I was expecting but I can say that it is a life that I have enjoyed. I have been very proud of every product or service that I've ever sold to a library, and I consider myself to be lucky for that. And I have taken great pride in forming myself into the kind of salesperson that I would like to have call on me.

The Future

» Now, more than ever, sales is about the big picture rather than a one-item sale

» Salespeople need to be constantly aware of organizational changes and adapt offerings accordingly

» Your products and services must play well with others

» There is always a place for light-heartedness and laughter

———— Epilogue ————

Long before I knew what an 856 field was, or about the Conspectus method, I learned that library vendors were bad. I did not personally know any vendor representatives when I was a student in library school, but I quickly received the impression there and in the early years of my librarian career that employees of library vendors were shallow, myopic, and uninterested in the mission of libraries. Over time, as I got to know and befriend professionals in the vendor and publishing world, my heart slowly began to thaw, and then I began to realize that what was going on "out there" in the world of publishing and library vendors directly impacted how well I could do my job as an academic librarian. And then one day I became a vendor myself. Overnight, everything about me seemed to change with some of my librarian colleagues. Jokes about heading to "the dark side" were among the more charitable comments I received, and I was genuinely surprised by how many of my librarian colleagues behaved in ways that led me to believe that somehow I had betrayed them, my profession, or both. After a while, I left my work as a vendor to return to work for a library consortium, not because I was unhappy there or because I had a Road to Damascus–like conversion, but because I realized that the world of library consortia is where my true passion lies—working at the crossroads of libraries and library vendors to shape mutually beneficial relationships between these two primary stakeholders in the dissemination of academic scholarship.

Even now, after I have returned to the academic library community and am assimilating back into my native culture, I still believe that a majority of librarians ignore or misconstrue what happens in the academic publishing community to their professional disadvantage. At a very simple level, I do not think many librarians appreciate the difficulty of their sales representatives' jobs, which is why I am proud of Jenni Wilson for speaking so candidly and humorously in her chapter. On a more complicated level, however, I think librarians cannot truly understand all the dynamics of our industry if they do not more often put themselves in the shoes of their vendors, as Robert Boissy and Rebecca Seger invite us to do in their excellent chapters. It is easy for someone to criticize vendors or suppliers in any industry, but I tend to think that if librarians found themselves working for vendors, they would often make the same decisions for which they so quickly criticize their vendors. The reverse is also likely true. We could all stand to be a little nicer to the other side.

I would recommend that librarians and publishers aspire to model the same relationship dynamics that firms have with their suppliers in other industries, for I believe the supplier/customer dynamics in play in the scholarly communication ecosystem should ideally behave no differently than those relationships in other industries. And no, I do not believe that is too aspirational of a goal. I am struck by the fact, however, that our industry often does not behave in a consistently mature, mutually beneficial manner. Library users usually don't know or care about these relationships; instead, they want accurate, authoritative content that helps them with their research, teaching, or learning needs. Yet, too often, librarians believe they are the customers who most need to be made happy when, in fact, library users are the ones whose satisfaction should be paramount—within reason. Most publishers do not see librarians as their end users, instead seeing the student or researcher in that capacity, as the chapters from Steven Rhind-Tutt and Rolf Janke point out. As a librarian, I do not see this as a bad thing, but it does require librarians to view their professional relationships with publishers and other vendors in a much more symbiotic fashion. When a library patron is frustrated with a library resource, for example, their frustration is likely directed at their library far more frequently than it is directed at one of its suppliers. That's actually not surprising; if the transmission in my Toyota prematurely failed, I would be annoyed more by Toyota than I would be with one of its many suppliers, one of whom actually supplied Toyota with that faulty transmission. Key to assuming, embracing, and celebrating a symbiotic relationship is knowledge of each other, and hopefully this book will move that rock forward a few feet on that front.

Among the many themes these chapters have addressed, the two most important issues I hope librarians take away from reading this book are fairly simple. First, I hope librarians understand that if they are ever going to compete with publishers and "take back" a substantial portion of the scholarly communication market, they will need to understand the entire gamut of what it takes to be a successful publisher in the 21st century. As Mark Kendall, Jayne Marks, and Alison Mudditt describe in their chapters, so much of the business of running a publishing house does not actually keep the library at the forefront of day-to-day thinking. Steven Smith's chapter reveals that monograph publishing requires a strategic, proactive approach, and a publisher that is doing its job isn't merely sitting back and waiting to see what submissions come its way. Moreover, only when I became an employee of an academic publisher, for example, did I learn about the worlds Carol Richman and Barbara Walthall describe in their chapters. To be a successful publisher in a globalized world, then, takes much more work than simply adding articles to an institutional repository once reviewers have approved a submitted article manuscript. Second—and perhaps this is a more modest goal—I would hope that more librarians view the care and feeding of their suppliers as a noteworthy goal, and I hope this book helps librarians better understand the perspectives of the many different kinds of employees who work for academic publishers. In that capacity, therefore, understanding what makes a publisher tick and "how the sausage is made," so to speak, is a critically and often overlooked aspect of being a good information professional. Michael Levine-Clark's chapter makes this case very effectively, which is why we intentionally made it the first chapter in this book.

But I hope this book is also helpful for my colleagues in academic publishing. Too often employees of publishers get siloed into their own functional units and do not interact with or understand what is going on in other parts of their own organization. That is not good for publishers and it is not good for librarians. As a result, for example, sales professionals sometimes cannot adequately represent their company's guiding mission to their customers, for they function as little more than hired guns with little organizational loyalty, or editorial teams may not know what's actually going on in the minds of librarians, or customer service representatives may have little knowledge

of the products they troubleshoot. Academic publishers may be globally ori-
ented, but their ability to create organizations where their employees become
narrowly obsessed with their respective functional areas should not be left
unchallenged. Librarians need to know more about academic publishing, but
just as importantly, employees of publishers ironically also need to know more
about the holistic publishing cycle. Publishers need to realize that not every
library in the world needs their content, or at the very least, that in an environment with scarce financial resources, their content may not be as important to some libraries as is their competitors.'

When I was in high school, my school did what many schools do around
the country, and for one day each year our principal would trade places with
a randomly selected student. Our principal would spend his day attending
gym class, eating lunch in the cafeteria, and sitting through whatever classes
that particular student was taking. Meanwhile, the student with whom he
swapped places would make morning announcements, chair a faculty meeting, and perform a few of our principal's more mundane daily tasks. It was a
cute gimmick, of course, but nearly everyone loved it, and the participants of
this annual job swap always spoke of how much they learned about the other
party's perspective by having walked one day in that person's shoes.

I have often wondered if a similar gimmick would be helpful for our profession. Having worked in both library and library-vendor settings, I have
often thought that many employees of traditional library vendors would be
pretty bad librarians, and many librarians I know would fail miserably if they
had to work for a library vendor. Vendors could teach librarians how not to
get bogged down with organizational minutiae that prevent them from moving quickly enough to satisfy the fast-changing needs of most 21st-century
users, while librarians could teach vendors how to be better obsessed (and
proficient!) with customer service, and how to let an organization's long-term
mission guide their day-to-day work. Librarians often do an amazing job at
creating strategies that holistically meet their organization's and profession's
missions but struggle with the tactical implementation of those well-meaning
visions. Publishers and other library vendors strike me as the better tacticians
but often do a terrible job in communicating their strategies to the marketplace, change their strategies too often to align with a new management team,

or, even worse, have organizational missions that are not in the best interests of long-term, sustainable scholarship.

Some might argue that, like the pop-psychology romance guide from a few decades ago, librarians are from Venus and library vendors are from Mars. Indeed, it can occasionally feel this way at industry conferences, and I certainly received that impression throughout my graduate school training. My career's passion is to bring these two disparate planets together, because I actually do not think these parties need to feel separated by millions of miles of nonoxygenated space. Not only do I not believe that librarians and library vendors live on different planets, I believe they very much live on the same planet—and will only live well on that planet if they do a better job of acknowledging the other's existence on that same planet. Each side has a lot to learn from each other, and while this book has been directed primarily to an audience that has little experience with academic publishing, surely more work can be done in transparently peeling back the curtain on many of the often ignored aspects of our industry—this important planet we call scholarly communication that we have all chosen to inhabit. Hopefully, I have a number of years left in this profession to continue to work on these efforts, but perhaps this book is a good start.

James Wiser
Editor

Index